THE MAGNOLIA STORY

THE MAGNOLIA STORY

CHIP & JOANNA GAINES

with Mark Dagostino

W PUBLISHING GROUP

AN IMPRINT OF THOMAS NELSON

Published in Nashville, Tennessee, by W Publishing, an imprint of Thomas Nelson. W Publishing and Thomas Nelson are registered trademarks of HarperCollins Christian Publishing, Inc.

Thomas Nelson titles may be purchased in bulk for educational, business, fundraising, or sales promotional use. For information, please e-mail SpecialMarkets@ ThomasNelson.com.

Library of Congress Control Number: 2016945748

ISBN 978-0-7180-7918-5 (HC)
ISBN 978-0-7852-2051-0 (SC)
ISBN 978-0-7180-8153-9 (eBook)

Printed in the United States of America

20 21 22 23 LSC 6 5 4 3

We would like to dedicate this book to our children—Drake, Ella Rose, Emmie Kay, Duke, and Crew—and to the children of Restoration Gateway. Our commitment to you will never fade.

CONTENTS

BLESSINGS IN
(A BIG, UGLY) DISGUISE

I have always been one to play it safe. If it were up to me, the less risk involved the better. But this isn't how the story goes—because I am married to the one, the only, Chip Carter Gaines.

One day back in early 2012, my husband decided to go window-shopping online. That's always a risky thing to do, but when Chip's the man behind the mouse it can be downright dangerous. I never know what object—or animal—might show up at my front door on the back of some random delivery truck.

On this particular day, Chip happened to spot a used houseboat for sale.

We'd been living in a house that we were getting ready to flip and we'd just started renovating our farmhouse outside of Waco, Texas, which meant we were on the hunt for a temporary place to live. So Chip clicked through the pictures of that floating two-story shanty with its microscopic kitchen and had a full-blown Chip Gaines epiphany.

I really thought to myself, *How cool would it be to move our family onto a houseboat? We can put it on one of the lakes down here, and the kids and I can fish for breakfast from the balcony. Wow! Jo's gonna love this.*

So he bought it. Sight unseen. We just barely had our heads above water at that point, and he went and threw tens of thousands of dollars down on that thing. And then he didn't say a word. He had it shipped to Waco on a monster tractor-trailer and couldn't wait to show off his surprise when it finally arrived. After all our years of marriage, he was still clueless about how I might react.

I had no idea any of this was going on, of course. But right around that same time, on some random weeknight, I received a phone call from an out-of-state number I didn't recognize. I picked it up.

"Hi, I'm Katie Neff, and I work for a television production company," the woman on the line said. "I saw some of your designs online, and I was wondering . . ."

This Katie had apparently seen photos of our most recent flip house that I'd designed, the one we were living in at the time. A few weeks earlier a friend of mine, Molly, had submitted those photos to a popular blog called DesignMom.com, and I'd been excited that a blog with thousands of followers wanted to feature it. It was the first time my work had ever really been featured on a design blog other than my own. I had a loyal local following back then, but no national following to speak of.

"I loved what you did," Katie continued, "so I looked you up and read *your* blog too. I see that you and your husband work together, and I was just wondering: Would you ever want to be on a TV show?"

I sat there and thought, *Did I just hear that right?*

"What about us would you want to show on TV?" I asked.

"Well, we just love how organic it is—that you and your husband work together. Not only do you sell homes, but you also flip and renovate them. We think it's unique that you're a husband-and-wife team." She went on and on, and I finally said, "Well, let me talk to Chip and I'll get back with you."

I got with Chip, and he immediately said, "That's a scam. Don't call them back."

I was just skeptical. Back in high school I had some buddies who were always trying to get into modeling. They would go to these "agents" and "casting calls" and then wind up paying some guy $1,000 to take their headshots, and nothing would ever come of it. So, yeah, I thought it was something like that.

Jo really thought we should give them a shot, but I was just like, "Jo, I'm telling you, there's no way this is legit. We're gonna meet these people, and they'll get us all excited thinking they're gonna make us famous or something, and then say, 'Oh, by the way, you need to pay us twenty grand.'"

I somehow convinced Chip to let me call Katie back. We didn't have a lot of money just lying around, so I knew there was no way anyone could trick us out of thousands of dollars. (Of course, I knew nothing about that houseboat yet!)

Sure enough, within a couple of weeks Katie sent an entire camera crew to Waco to spend five days filming us for what they called a "sizzle reel"—basically an extended commercial they would put together to try to sell a television series based on the two of us and our little business. They never asked us for any money at all. They were legit, which made us wonder: Why in the world would anyone care to watch us on TV? We don't even *watch* TV. These people have to be nuts.

After the crew spent a couple of days with us, they started thinking they might be nuts too. Chip and I were *horrible*. We were scared of the cameras, which is hilarious because Chip is the most talkative guy I know. But like clockwork, the moment that red light turned on, he froze.

My mouth was all dry and I couldn't think straight, and Jo was a little dull. They just followed Jo around and tried to make something out of nothing. It was pretty obvious this could not make good television. We were just awful. We really were.

The crew had me stand in my kitchen and try to make pancakes with the kids hanging off of my legs while Chip was basically sucking his thumb over in the corner, and the whole time I was trying to convince the kids not to look into the camera so it would look more "natural." It certainly didn't *feel* natural, and it definitely wasn't any fun.

On the fourth day, just before the camera crew was scheduled to go home, their top guy pulled us aside and said, "Look, if something doesn't happen here, there's no way you guys are getting a show. This just isn't working."

We figured we were pretty much done at that point, and it didn't really bother us at all. The two of us had never imagined we'd be on TV. We'd talked to friends about the kinds of things they watched on "reality TV," and from what we could tell, none of it seemed like us anyway.

Then something happened. The very next morning, the houseboat arrived. With cameras rolling, Chip put a blindfold on me and drove me to an empty lot by the lake.

With all cameras on me, Chip released the blindfold and said, "Ta-da!"

I wasn't sure what I was looking at. A shipwreck, maybe? On the back of a semi?

"What is that?" I said.

"I got this for you, Jo!" Chip replied.

"That *better* not be for me," I said. It was the ugliest, rundown-looking, two-story shack of a boat I'd ever seen. "What the heck are we going to do with a houseboat?"

"That's our new home!" Chip said, beaming with pride at his purchase.

"What? You are crazy. We are not living on a houseboat."

It quickly dawned on me that this wasn't a joke and Chip wasn't even close to kidding. I wasn't mishearing him. He was dead serious about making that boat our home for the next six months.

I just about lost it. "How can we live on the water, Chip? Three of our kids don't even know how to swim! Did you think this through?!"

Then he fessed up and told me how much money he'd spent on it. As it all sank in, I realized I'd never been so mad at him—ever—and that's saying something.

"Come on. At least come look at it. I know this can work," he pleaded.

As soon as we walked a little closer, we could see the holes. *Holes*. In the *boat*.

We pulled ourselves up onto the flatbed and went inside to find the interior covered in mold. Someone had taken the AC unit out on top and left a gaping hole in the roof, so for years it had rained straight into the boat. We tried turning the engine over, and of course it didn't start. That's when Chip got angry. "I think I got scammed," he said.

"Chip, did you even look at this thing before you bought it?"

"Well, no," he said. "It was a great deal, and there were all kinds of pictures. It looked like it was in great shape. Oh, wait a minute. I bet the guy just put up pictures of this thing from when he bought it, like in 1980 or something. That sorry sucker."

"Sorry sucker? Chip . . ."

By this point I'm trying to decide if we could scrap it for parts. My husband had made plenty of impulsive purchases. That's just what he does. He'd gone and purchased the house we were currently in without showing that to me, either. But at least it was a house, with a roof, on a foundation. I'd gone along with it, as I always do, and over time I'd come to love that quirky shoe box of a house.

We had worked hard to make it our home. In fact, that house is where I'd had my epiphany about truly owning the space you're in (a moment I'll share with you later in this book) and where I'd designed the kids' rooms that landed on the blog and caused the producer to call. I was already pretty upset that we were going to have to leave that house behind in a few months. But to think that we might have to move into this . . . *thing* was just too much.

"You need to return it," I said.

"It's paid for," Chip said. "It's done. I bought it as is."

"Excuse me, semi driver!" I yelled to the man in the front seat.

"I need you to hook that thing back up and take it back where it came from!"

Chip made it clear to me that once he made a deal—fair or not—that thing was ours now.

By that point the cameras had totally disappeared to both of us. We just completely forgot they were there. Chip's arms were flailing around as he circled the boat, tallying up the problems he could find. My arms were flailing as I yelled at him for buying that dumb thing without talking to me first.

When I finally calmed down, I saw how disappointed he was and how bad he felt. I decided to take a deep breath and try to think this thing through.

"Maybe it's not that bad," I said. (I think I was trying to cheer myself up as much as I was trying to console Chip.) "If we fix up the interior and just get it to the point where we can get it onto the water, at least maybe then we can turn around, sell it, and get our money back."

Over the course of the next hour or so, I really started to come around. I took another walk through the boat and started to picture how we could make it livable—maybe even kind of cool. After all, we'd conquered worse. We tore a few things apart right then and there, and I grabbed some paper and sketched out a new layout for the tiny kitchen. I talked to him about potentially finishing an accent wall with shiplap—a kind of rough-textured pine paneling that fans of our show now know all too well.

"*Ship*lap?" Chip laughed. "That seems a little ironic to use on a *ship*, doesn't it?"

"Ha-ha," I replied. I was still not in the mood for his jokes, but this is how Chip backs me off the ledge—with his humor.

Then I asked him to help me lift something on the deck, and he said, "Aye, aye, matey!" in his best pirate voice, and slowly but surely I came around.

I can't believe I'm saying this, but by the end of that afternoon I was actually a little bit excited about taking on such a big challenge. Chip was still deflated that he'd allowed himself to get duped, but he put his arm around me as we started walking back to the truck. I put my head on his shoulder. And the cameras captured the whole thing— just an average, roller-coaster afternoon in the lives of Chip and Joanna Gaines.

The head cameraman came jogging over to us before we drove away. Chip rolled down his window and said sarcastically, "How's *that* for reality TV?" We were both feeling embarrassed that this is how we had spent our last day of trying to get this stinkin' television show.

"Well," the guy said, breaking into a great big smile, "if I do my job, you two just landed yourself a reality TV show."

What? We were floored. We couldn't believe it. How was *that* a show? But lo and behold, he was right. That rotten houseboat turned out to be a blessing in disguise. Over the course of the next few months, the production company's head of development, Patrick Jager, championed our show tirelessly—until HGTV decided we were just what they wanted. Apparently one of the big selling points was the "authenticity" we'd shown during that humbling afternoon. We couldn't have scripted it even if we'd tried. There was something about Chip's impulsiveness, his riskiness, combined with my reaction to his riskiness and the way we worked it out as a couple, that landed us the show.

A few months later, the cameras were back—and *Fixer Upper* was born. Our quiet little lives turned completely upside down as our life's work became a hit TV show. After years of toiling away semi-anonymously here in Waco, trying to make ends meet while designing our clients' dream homes and doing our best to raise our four kids right, our world changed in a way that was much different than either of us ever could have imagined.

Now that we've had some time to reflect on it, it's as if our whole lives had been preparing us for this experience. We didn't know it at the time, but it's as if the seeds had been planted long ago.

Have you ever looked at the bud of a magnolia flower? It's a tight little pod that stays closed up for a long time on the end of its branch until one day, out of nowhere, it finally bursts open into this gigantic, gorgeous, fragrant flower that's ten times bigger than the bud itself. It's impossible to imagine that such a big beautiful thing could pop out of that tiny little bud. But it does. And that's sort of what getting "discovered" and sharing our lives on *Fixer Upper* feels like to us.

We never could have imagined being on TV together, touching the lives of so many people, especially back when we were two broke newly-weds sleeping on the floor of our eight-hundred-square-foot house while we renovated it, or when I first opened and then had to *close* my little Magnolia shop on Bosque Boulevard. I have to wonder, though, if it was just a happy coincidence that we decided to name that shop Magnolia. Or was it something more? Because it's staggering to think just how much it has blossomed.

As we finished up writing this book, HGTV was airing the third season of *Fixer Upper,* and we'd started filming seasons four and five. And that's only part of the excitement. Thanks to the show's popularity, we outgrew our beloved "Little Shop on Bosque." In 2015, to make room for all our new customers, we moved the shop into a converted, early twentieth-century cotton-oil mill. Our new property is marked by two giant, rusty, abandoned silos in the heart of downtown Waco—easy to spot from miles away. It's a place where we're proud to welcome our out-of-town visitors.

To get how exciting this is for us, you have to understand where it all started: a little shop, one employee, and a shopgirl who was happy to see eight customers a day. The reality that thousands of visitors are coming to our town to experience Magnolia Market at the Silos is not only an honor, it's one of the single greatest accomplishments of our careers.

We've also had the great thrill of seeing our friends' businesses boom, since we've gotten to incorporate their work and artistry into the shop and the show. That was our goal from the beginning—to bless our community, our friends, and our viewers through this unbelievable platform we've been given.

Chip and I have received generous opportunities to speak all over the country, to give DIY tips on talk shows, to design our own furniture, rug and paint lines, and now to write a book. A book! Can you believe it?

For the two of us, writing these pages has offered a welcome chance to stop and look back on the story of our lives, and it certainly has been an eye-opening process. How many of us take the time to relive half a lifetime's worth of happy memories, cringeworthy failures, and unforgettable adventures together? How many of us get a chance to sit down and talk about the rough times we overcame in the past or to laugh about the stupid mistakes we made when we were young?

Working on this book has allowed us to look back on all the things that brought us here to the farm, to this place we love so much, and to this busy, exciting season in our lives. And let me tell you, it's been one heck of a journey. We're still trying to figure out how to make this new life work for us and our kids, smack-dab in the middle of these exciting new adventures we've been on. Writing it all down has also allowed us to reflect on the inspiration we've picked up and the lessons we've learned along the way—and there have been many!

We feel so blessed to be able to share all of this with you in the hope that you'll find new ways to love the space and season you're in too.

Even after all of this thinking and talking and writing, Chip and I still look at each other at the end of the day and say, "Us? Really?" Honestly, we're still pretty baffled as to why people seem to like watching the two of us be "us" on national TV, because these are the same old things we've been doing since the very day we met. But that's a story for another chapter.

FIRST DATES AND
SECOND CHANCES

To this day, I am still not sure what it was about Chip Gaines that made me give him a second chance—because, basically, our first date was over before it even started.

I was working at my father's Firestone automotive shop the day we first met. I'd worked as my dad's office manager through my years at Baylor University and was perfectly happy working there afterward while I tried to figure out what I really wanted to do with my life. The smell of tires, metal, and grease—that place was like a second home to me, and the guys in the shop were all like my big brothers.

On this particular afternoon, they all started teasing me. "You should go out to the lobby, Jo. There's a hot guy out there. Go talk to him!" they said.

"No," I said. "Stop it! I'm not doing that."

I was all of twenty-three, and I wasn't exactly outgoing.

She was a bit awkward—no doubt about that.

I hadn't dated all that much, and I'd never had a serious relationship—nothing that lasted longer than a month or two. I'd always been an introvert and still am (believe it or not). I was also very picky, and I just wasn't the type of girl who struck up conversations with guys I didn't know. I was honestly comfortable being single; I didn't think that much of it.

"Who is this guy, anyway?" I asked, since they all seemed to know him for some reason.

"Oh, they call him Hot John," someone said, laughing.

Hot John? There was no *way* I was going out in that lobby to strike up a conversation with some guy called Hot John. But the guys wouldn't let up, so I finally said, "Fine."

I gathered up a few things from my desk (in case I needed a backup plan) and rounded the corner into the lobby. I quickly realized that Hot John *was* pretty good-looking. He'd obviously just finished a workout—he was dressed head-to-toe in cycling gear and was just standing there, innocently waiting on someone from the back. I tried to think about what I might say to strike up a conversation when I got close enough and quickly settled on the obvious topic: cycling. But just as that thought raced through my head, he looked up from his magazine and smiled right at me.

Crap, I thought. I completely lost my nerve. I kept on walking right past him and out the lobby's front door.

When I reached the safety of my dad's outdoor waiting area, I realized just how bad I'd needed the fresh air. I sat on a chair a few down from another customer and immediately started laughing at myself. *Did I really just do that?*

"Hey, what's so funny?" the customer sitting near me asked.

I looked up at him, and before I could even answer he asked, "Wait, aren't you the girl from the commercials?"

"Yeah, that's me," I said, still embarrassed from my awkward encounter with Hot John. I was, in fact, the girl from the commercials. I had some interest in television news. I had even done an internship with CBS in New York City, working under Dan Rather in the news division, and because of that my dad had insisted I go on camera for the local TV ads he ran for his shop.

I was so caught up in my own thoughts that I didn't even get a good look at this guy who had started talking to me. He was wearing a baseball cap and seemed like an average customer. He seemed around my age, maybe a bit older—that was all I really noticed. What did strike me was that he was real chatty, so we wound up sitting there for twenty minutes just shooting the breeze.

Over the course of our conversation, he told me he was a Baylor grad. That struck me as odd. The guys I'd known at Baylor were more the clean-cut type. This guy seemed a little rough-and-tumble, the kind who'd rather work with his hands than keep a corporate calendar. But right off the bat I could tell he was smart—and definitely hardworking. He was just at the shop getting the brakes fixed on his truck. I also found it interesting that he'd stuck around Waco after graduation. "I love this town," he said. "I'm planning to stay in Waco until God makes it clear I'm supposed to move on."

That surprised me too. I loved the way he mentioned God in a way that was so unguarded, and I liked that he wanted to stay in Waco. That was rare for Baylor grads. Normally people shipped themselves straight off to the big cities after graduation.

Speaking of, that whole week I had been debating whether or not to move back to New York City to pursue my dream of broadcast journalism. Most of my friends and family were encouraging me to go, and I was really wrestling with it. It occurred to me this could be my one big chance, but I also really liked it right where I was.

All of a sudden Hot John walked out and said, "Hey, Chip, let's go." I was confused. The man I'd been chatting with—who apparently was named Chip—explained that John was his roommate and that they were business partners. Oh, *of course* these two had come together. I was still completely embarrassed about my initial encounter with Hot John, but I said, "Hi." And then, thankfully, this Chip went right back to our conversation as Hot John took a seat and joined in.

Chip asked me about New York and what I wanted to do, and how long my dad had owned the shop, and what it was I loved about Waco.

He asked about my sisters and my family in general, and what I'd done at Baylor, and if I'd known a few communications majors he'd run around with at school. (I told y'all he was chatty!) Somehow none of these questions seemed intrusive or strange to me at the time, which is funny, because thinking back I find them particularly telling.

At the time, it was just like talking with an old friend.

John finally stood up, and this baseball-cap-wearing customer that John had introduced as Chip followed. "Well, nice talking to you," he said.

"Nice talking to you too," I replied, and that was it. I went back inside. The guys in the shop wanted to know what I thought about Hot John, and I just laughed. "Sorry, guys, I don't think it's gonna work out."

The next day I came back from my lunch break to find a note on my desk: "Chip Gaines called. Call him back." I thought, *Oh, that must be the guy I met yesterday.* So I called him. I honestly thought he was going to ask me about getting a better price on his brakes or something, but instead he said, "Hey, I really enjoyed our conversation yesterday. I was wondering . . . you want to go out sometime?"

And for some reason I said okay—just like that, without any hesitation. It wasn't like me at all. When I hung up the phone, I went, "What in the world just happened!"

So you said okay immediately? I don't even remember that. That's fun! No reservations? Man, I must've been good-lookin'.

What Chip didn't know was I didn't even give myself time to have reservations. Something told me to just go for it.

Cute, Joey. This story makes me love you all over again.

My parents were out of town that week, but I remember calling to tell them, "I'm going on a date with a customer that was in getting his brakes done. I met him yesterday." I guess it's unusual for a twenty-three-year-old to call her parents and tell them she's going on a date, but it was normal for me. I was extremely close to my parents and I was just excited to tell them.

My parents and my little sister, Mary Kay, whom I call Mikey, asked me what this Chip guy looked like, and I said, "I honestly can't tell you. He had a baseball cap on, and the way we were sitting, I didn't really get a good look at him."

When the night of our big date came, I was giddy and a bit anxious. I got ready at my sister's apartment. She and her roommates, Sarah and Katiegh, were all there for moral support, and Chip was supposed to pick me up at six. Six rolls around. No Chip. Then six thirty—still no Chip. I thought, *Well, maybe he thought the date was at seven*, so I gave him the benefit of the doubt. But when seven came and went, I was officially done.

Finally, at seven thirty, a full ninety minutes late, he knocked at the door.

"Don't even answer it," I whispered to my friends. "I don't want to go anywhere with this idiot."

"But we want to see what he looks like!" they said, and so one of them finally opened the door while I hung back out of sight.

"Well, hello, ladies," Chip said as he pushed his way into the apartment. I could tell that he charmed every one of them in about two seconds flat. I finally decided to step out and at least take a look at him. He was not like I remembered at all. This guy had no hair. I'd imagined he had hair under the baseball cap, but nope. Just stubble. And his face was weathered and flushed red, like he'd been working outside in the hot sun all day long. He was wearing a reddish-toned leather jacket, too, and I thought, *Is this red guy even the same guy I was talking to at the shop?*

It turned out that Chip had shaved his head to support a friend of his who was battling cancer.

A bunch of us shaved our heads for a good friend of mine. It was growing back, but it was just about a buzz cut at that point.

I still don't remember what he said that convinced me to walk out the door with him. He didn't even have a plan for our date. He said, "So, Joanna, where do you want to go eat?" He didn't apologize for being late, either. He had so much confidence. I don't know. I can't explain it. Only Chip could be an hour and a half late and have no one mad about it.

I wasn't an hour and a half late. She's making that up. I was, like, twenty minutes late.

Chip was an hour and a half late to *everything*. If I'd known that then, maybe I wouldn't have taken it personally.

Well, I think you're wrong. You're cute, though, and you do have me on the no-plans thing. That was bad. I don't know why I'm like that. I just never have any plans. I like the way things just work themselves out. It's more fun that way. I wasn't nervous about the date or where to eat, and I wasn't nervous about being late.

Out in his truck, Chip asked me again where I'd like to eat, so I suggested a place out in Valley Mills, a small town about thirty minutes from Waco—which, looking back, was a gutsy move for a first date. Thirty minutes was a long time to be in a car if you ran out of things to talk about. But there was a restaurant there in a historic mansion where my parents liked to go. It was really charming, and it was the first place that popped into my head.

The whole drive over there was kind of like a dream. Jo wasn't anything like the girls I typically went out with. But she was so cute, you know? We wound up driving out of town through these back roads—I didn't know where in the heck we were going—and we came up to this mansion with pillars on the front that looked like something you'd see in *Gone with the Wind*.

Everything was going about like I'd expected until we sat down at the table and the owner of the restaurant came over. Everywhere I went in Waco and Dallas, someone was always coming up and talking to me, so I thought maybe this guy was coming over to say hello. Turns out he wasn't coming to talk to me at all. He was coming over to talk to Joanna.

"Hey, sweetheart, how are you? I saw your latest commercial. Tell your mom and dad I said hello, okay?" They talked for quite a while, and my mind started turning, like, *Wow. This girl is a local superstar.*

Dinner was perfect. We were both comfortable with each other for some reason, and the conversation came easy. When the bill came, Chip quickly popped up and took a big roll of cash out of his pocket. I don't think I'd ever seen anyone carry that much cash. My dad was successful, but he kept his money in a bank. Seeing that, I thought, *Oh, that's why he stayed in Waco. He's doing really well for himself!*

You thought I was rich. Ha! What you didn't know is that was probably all the money I had in the world. I always carried cash. I'd carry, like, $1,000 on me in those days. I just loved the way it felt. Plus, I worked with a lot of rough dudes, and some of them expected to be paid in cash.

It's funny because I went to Baylor, where I was surrounded by all these rich kids from rich families, and for whatever reason I was never drawn to that. I was much more comfortable hanging out with the guys who dug ditches. I lived like them, too, whether it was carrying all my money around in my pocket or sitting under some shady tree at lunchtime while they laughed at me trying to eat jalapeños.

After dinner the two of us went and sat on that grand front porch for a while. It was a beautiful night, and I could have just sat there and listened to the silence. But Chip, of course—he had other ideas. I just looked at him until I couldn't even hear him anymore. I remember thinking, *Nope. This guy isn't even close to done.*

In my head, I started to go down the checklist we women put together in our heads and our hearts. I'd always been attracted to people with dark hair. He was blond or redheaded or something in between—it was too short to tell. I would have preferred hair, period.

I'd always been attracted to quiet guys, too, which I knew was a problem because the quiet guys never had the nerve to ask me out, and they certainly never drew me out the way this guy did. Still, he was all over the place. He was talking about the businesses he'd started, and these ideas he had, and how he was buying up little houses and flipping them and renting some out to Baylor students, and I was wondering if he was just a bit crazy.

I liked stability. I liked safety. I liked *traditional* and I liked being on time. And this Chip with the beet-red face wasn't any of those things. I did think he was kind of fascinating, though.

I know this is going to sound strange to some people, but right in the middle of that—right in the middle of me trying to figure this guy out—a little voice in my head said, *That's the man you're going to marry.* I swear to you it was clear as day. It seemed like the voice of God, or maybe it was some deep intuition, but I heard it. In fact, I heard it so loudly that I completely tuned out our conversation and lost focus.

My roommates asked me a million questions after he dropped me off that night: "What was he like? Did he try to kiss you? How was the date?" And my response was that it was good. We had fun. He was a good talker. And no, he didn't try to kiss me. I didn't tell them about that voice in my head. It seemed far too ridiculous. But honestly, if it wasn't for that voice, I'm not sure I would have stuck it out through all the ups and downs of dating a guy like Chip. I was spinning a bit, but I certainly didn't fall instantly head-over-heels for him or anything like that.

It wasn't exactly a love at first sight for me, either. It was a fun date, but I'd been on lots of fun dates. Something was different, though. Joanna impressed me. I couldn't stop thinking about that owner coming up to talk to her. I was honestly the one who normally got the attention. She was totally different from the typical blonde-haired, blue-eyed cheerleader type I tended to date. But the more I thought about her, the more I knew I wanted to see her again.

We made plans to go get coffee the following week, but I had to cancel. I hurt my back. In fact, I needed to go into the hospital for surgery, and I let Chip know that. He seemed real concerned and wished me luck—and then he didn't call me again. He didn't send flowers to the hospital. Nothing.

Flowers to the hospital? After one date?

Yes! That would've been the chivalrous thing to do. Everyone thought it was rude that you didn't call after that.

Huh. Well, I apologize, Jo. I didn't even think about that.

It's okay. I forgive you. I think it turned out okay in the end.

Even though he wasn't what I'd pictured as the type of man I might be interested in, there was just something about Chip Gaines that I couldn't get off my mind. I kept thinking about him—and thinking about just how weird it all was.

Our first date happened at the end of October, and it wasn't until after the turn of the New Year—early January something—that I finally got another phone call from him.

"Hey, Jo, I just wanted to say that I really enjoyed our date, and I think we ought to stop playing all these games," he said.

I was sitting there thinking, *What games is this guy talking about?*

I'd made a bet with Hot John to see who could hold out the longest before calling our dates back. I really wanted that fifty dollars from John! That's the only reason I didn't call.

I think Chip was still dating a few girls off and on then.

Yeah, I think you're right. But I did want to win that fifty dollars, and it was killing me because I kept thinking about you and I really did think you were going to call any day now!

"There's a basketball game tonight. Would you like to go?" Chip asked me. Once again, without hesitation, I said yes, and from that night on, Chip and I started seeing each other almost every day. He would come by the tire shop to visit. He met my parents. I met his parents. I went out and drove around with him to see some of the properties he worked on and to meet some of the guys he worked with in his landscaping business. One guy, Melesio, was like a brother to Chip. I had never seen someone bond so closely to the people he worked with.

After a while, I even offered to help him do some of the books for the little businesses he was running, and he took me up on it. I'd never been around that kind of work before, but I thought it was fun. I thought *he* was fun.

About four months into it, we were shooting hoops in my dad's driveway when Chip stopped in his tracks, held me in his arms, looked into my eyes under the starry sky, and said, "I love you."

And I looked at him and said, "Thank you."

"Thank you?" Chip said.

I know I should have said, "I love you too," but this whole thing had been such a whirlwind, and I was just trying to process it all. No guy had ever told me he loved me before, and here Chip was saying it after what seemed like such a short period of time.

Chip got angry. He grabbed his basketball from under my arm and went storming off with it like a four-year-old.

I really thought, *What in the world is with this girl? I just told her I loved her, and that's all she can say?* It's not like I just went around saying that to people all the time. So saying it was a big deal for me too. But now I was stomping down the driveway going, *Okay, that's it. Am I dating an emotionless cyborg or something? I'm going home.*

Chip took off in his big, white Chevy truck with the Z71 stickers on the side, even squealing his tires a bit as he drove off, and it really sank in what a big deal that must have been for him. I felt bad—so bad that I actually got up the courage to call him later that night. I explained myself, and he said he understood, and by the end of the phone call we were right back to being ourselves.

Two weeks later, when Chip said, "I love you" again, I responded, "I love you too." There was no hesitation. I knew I loved him, and I knew it was okay to say so.

I'm not sure why I ever gave him a second chance when he showed up ninety minutes late for our first date or why I gave him another second chance when he didn't call me for two months after that. And I'm not sure why he gave me a second chance after I blew that romantic moment in the driveway. But I'm very glad I did, and I'm very glad he did too—because sometimes second chances lead to great things.

All of my doubts, all of the things I thought I wanted out of a relationship, and many of the things I thought I wanted out of life itself turned out to be just plain wrong. Instead? That voice from our first date turned out to be the thing that was absolutely right.

TWO

NEW DIRECTIONS

The first year Chip and I dated turned out to be my year of letting go—letting go of the notion that my life was going to be predictable in any way, shape, or form.

By his midtwenties, Chip had already been through a whole series of different businesses. Every time I thought I'd heard it all, he would tell me about something else that he'd done to earn a buck.

Like in college, I sold Scantron test forms. Those are the answer cards you use when taking certain kinds of tests. The teachers were able to run them through machines, and that sped up the grading process. Students at Baylor had to buy and bring their own Scantron forms to class with them, but hardly anyone ever remembered to do it. So before a test, the teacher would sit up at the front and say, "Who didn't bring their Scantron?" Two-thirds of the class would raise their hands, and she would sell them Scantron forms for two dollars apiece. This was kind of a slap on the wrist, so-to-speak, because at the bookstore they only cost, like, a dime each.

I went to the bookstore and bought a whole bunch of these things, and the next time she offered to sell some, I stood up and said, "Mine are only a dollar." I had so many people buy a Scantron that day, I walked away feeling pretty good about it. After all, I was a business major. I thought that move should've earned me an instant A.

I also sold books for a company called Southwestern Book Company for two summers in college. It was a program where you were sent to a town, usually pretty far from home. Your first objective was to convince people you'd never met to put you up for the summer—for free! And then you'd walk around town selling books door-to-door.

I'll tell you—that job changed my perspective as a college student. If you sold a lot of books you could pocket a lot of money, and because of the setup, you had really low overhead. The downside was that it was a ton of work, and it was far from home. Most kids weren't willing to do that.

I only spent about three dollars a day on a sandwich and some eggs, so all of the money I made went into my pocket. If I'd been a lifeguard or if I had waited tables over the summers, I would have wound up going out with my buddies and spending half my pay jacking around. But doing that program was almost like being sent to an island somewhere where all you do is work and sleep. And I was good at it.

I remember reading about work on Alaskan fishing boats where, if things worked out, you could earn north of $6,000 a month. It was grueling, potentially deadly stuff, but with no overhead, the money was all yours. These were the kinds of things I'd sit and think about while I was in class. I realized most people don't want to do what it takes to do a lot of things. I made up my mind right then and there—I would do whatever it takes to be successful.

The second summer, in the middle of selling books, I went to east Texas to open a fireworks stand. You can only sell fireworks in Texas during the two weeks before the Fourth of July, so I took the money I'd earned from half a summer's worth of bookselling and bought a fireworks stand and inventory. This probably seemed like a bonehead move to my parents, but I'd heard there was good money in it.

My friend Eric and I went in on the stand together. And it was not easy—no doubt about that—but I learned a lot. It was my first experience with investing. I did that the next two summers as well, opening three or four stands in east Texas, and my friend's uncle, whom I call Uncle Ricky, played a huge role in all of that. From selling books I knew I enjoyed hard work and the thrill of selling, but it was Uncle Ricky who recognized the entrepreneur in me and encouraged me to follow that dream.

There was something about the way Ricky would say, "Chip, you can do this," that made me believe I could. He really believed in me and trained me to some extent about simple business practices like paying taxes or understanding assets versus liabilities.

I took all that experience and used it to open up a lawn-mowing business, which quickly expanded into a full landscaping business with employees, equipment, and clients. Then I got the idea to buy some cheap properties on Third Street in Waco—sort of on the other side of the tracks, so to speak, but within a mile or so of the Baylor campus—so I could rent them out to incoming college students.

I was rocking and rolling. I wasn't inventing Facebook or anything like that, but I was definitely what you would call a serial entrepreneur.

Chip's experimentation with lots of different kinds of businesses had eventually evolved into flipping houses. By the time we met, he'd successfully done it for a few years. Flipping seemed to be his thing. I have to say it quickly became my favorite venture of his too.

When explaining to my friends and family what Chip did, I was always a little at a loss. He wasn't a realtor—at least people would've been able to understand that—and I'd never known a career could be made out of buying and selling houses. So even though I spent a lot of my time with Chip kind of playing catch-up to understand it all, it was exciting to me.

As I said before, Chip was a smart guy. Unconventional, maybe, but he always had the entrepreneurial spirit and business sense to back it up. I was intrigued by this lifestyle of his, maybe because it was wildly different from the "safe" world I'd grown up in. Every day seemed to bring a new adventure, because Chip really did refuse to be put in the nine-to-five box people filed themselves into after college graduation.

Even when things got complicated, Chip remained fearless. It seemed as if nothing could stop him, and I was hooked. I think that's why, when we were first dating in our twenties, we were doing things most people our age weren't doing.

Before he ever graduated from college, Chip had already figured out the game—banking, negotiations, selling, all of it. Most people in college are studying and dating, and Chip was certainly doing his fair share of that. But mostly he spent his time thinking, *What's the next business I can get into?* In that regard, he was kind of a step ahead of a lot of our peers.

By the time I started helping him with his properties, Chip was known as the unofficial "Mayor of Third Street." He owned a bunch of tiny little houses along this stretch of road that was also home to a school for troubled youth. Before he came in and fixed up some of the old houses to rent to Baylor students, a lot of people in Waco just steered clear of Third Street. But Chip was his fearless self and saw the area as a spot full of underpriced properties with potential.

The kids at the school were young, and there was something about that age group that made Chip think he still had time to make a difference. He would cruise up and down that street on his four-wheeler, checking on the progress at his various properties and checking in to make sure the tenants didn't need anything, and when he saw those kids walking by after school, he'd get into conversations and joke around with them.

He wound up convincing a few of those kids to help out doing lawns and odd jobs on the properties he owned, and he paid them well, which ended up making him a pretty popular guy with them. It seemed that every time he'd give one a job, four more would show up the next day, ready to earn a little money. It was inspiring to watch him work and to see how well he got along with everyone from his crew to his clients to those kids to Uncle Ricky, whom he introduced me to early on.

An interesting side note: Ricky and his wife made a hobby of importing antiques from Europe. They turned their little backyard into an absolute oasis full of old metal and wooden architectural pieces that he built into the landscape, and every time we went over there the backyard had some new feature added to it. It was like walking from an ordinary Texas front porch into an exotic vacation every time you walked out the back door. I remember thinking, even back then, *I would love to do something like that someday.*

So when Chip asked me to help him out that first summer we were dating, as he repainted and generally got his properties fixed up before the new Baylor students arrived in the fall, I was happy to do it. I didn't know anything about interior design or construction—I'd been a communications major, for heaven's sake—but I was more than content being his gofer.

To be honest, I didn't know any more about interior design or construction than Jo did. I learned it all on the fly. If I needed to put a fence in—or anything else, for that matter—I would just get my hands dirty and figure it out. Everything I did was that way. Story of my life!

I was still working at my dad's shop, too, but it was fun for me to see Chip's collection of little houses get all cleaned up. I liked thinking about the students who would soon be living in them and remembering what it had felt like to move into my first apartment. I wanted to make sure everything was right for those kids.

Most of the houses weren't much bigger than eight hundred square feet, so there wasn't a lot to work with, but I quickly saw how new carpet or a fresh paint color could change the whole atmosphere in a house that small. I liked the feeling of getting these jobs done and then watching the way those kids and their parents would go nuts as they were moving in.

There was something rewarding about that kind of work. Even if it was something as simple as painting one room, each project had a beginning, middle, and end. You could stand back and actually see what you'd accomplished at the end of the day, and there was something very satisfying in that for me—on top of how much fun it was just to watch Chip do his thing and try to imagine what he might do next.

It was more than just business. With Chip, it was everything. He was wild at heart, really. If you tried to give him a rule, he would break it. If you gave Chip a boundary, he would cross it.

Chip was just Chip. There was no box for this guy.

There's this movie, *Legends of the Fall*, where the character named Tristan goes off into these wild places. I've always thought of myself as kind of like that.

And (case in point) the things that would come out of his mouth were unlike anything anyone else would ever think to say. Sometimes it would take me a second to figure out whether he was joking around or drop-dead serious. He kept me on my toes—and I liked it.

Chip was also extremely kind and giving. I swear every time we'd see a homeless guy, Chip would stop and talk to him. Sometimes he'd give him money. Sometimes he'd give him a job for the day. Heck, if the weather was bad, he'd even put him up in a hotel.

We'd be walking downtown, and I'd hear, "Chip. Hey, Chip!" and I'd turn to see a person approaching us who, frankly, might have scared me if I was walking downtown by myself. Chip wouldn't be scared. He'd know the guy by name: "James! How's it going, brother?" It seemed as if every homeless guy in Waco knew Chip Gaines.

On the flip side, every banker in Waco knew Chip too. And he talked to those two very different groups of people exactly the same way. There was never any difference in Chip's demeanor. His enthusiasm for life and work and people was just infectious, and he surprised me with it again and again. At least once a day I caught myself thinking, *Wow, this guy!*

Best of all, as happy as Chip Gaines was, he seemed happiest around me.

I'm a generally happy person. My mom says I was a happy baby. But it's a fact—I was always happiest around Jo. And I still am.

One pretty amazing thing we learned early on was that the more time we spent together, the better our relationship was. I think a lot of couples feel the need to get away from each other now and then, to take little breaks, and they come back after a girls' weekend or a guys' fishing trip or something all refreshed and happy to reconnect because they missed each other.

We were just the opposite, and still are. We seem to give each other energy. We function better together than we do apart, and I don't think either one of us has ever felt the urge to say, "I need a break from you."

Don't get me wrong; we've certainly had our share of disappointment and arguments, but we just always wanted to tackle our issues together.

The two of us never talked about marriage during that first year we were together, but I knew pretty quickly that we were in this for the long haul, and I almost had to convince myself that it was okay to be in love with this man. I kept reminding myself, "With Chip, my life isn't gonna look like what I thought it was gonna look like—but there *will* be adventure, and there *will* be some fun."

My parents were the type of people who locked their doors and had an alarm system. For my whole life they encouraged me to go after what

I wanted, to get a good education, even to go to New York for that internship. But they also encouraged me to use caution—and I did.

Chip was the polar opposite. For example, whenever we went out shopping or to restaurants, he would leave his keys in the car. Who leaves their keys in the car in today's world? It was a real problem for us for a while, because my first instinct when I got out of the car was to lock the doors. So we'd come back after dinner and realize I'd locked Chip's keys in the car again.

I remember that! In college, I would not only leave my keys in the car, but half the time I would forget and leave it running.

What's ironic about Jo and my parents is Jo's parents were pretty much hippies in their younger years. Her dad served in Vietnam, and he was this tall, quiet, lanky guy with glasses, and her mom was this vivacious Korean woman who just loved life. They both have the best stories. When I first saw pictures of the two of them from before Jo was born, they looked like John Lennon and Yoko Ono. They were right in the thick of all that went on during the sixties. But despite that youthful "rebellion," they turned out to be the kind of cautious parents who were concerned with traditions and playing it safe.

My parents both grew up in a little bitty town called Archer City, Texas, and they were straight as an arrow, but they left the garage door open all day, even when they were out. They wouldn't even think about locking the doors. My mom saw an upside to everything, and I think that's part of what made me so optimistic and adventurous.

I have to say, I'm very thankful that Jo's parents were all right with us being together. They could have said, "This guy is not gonna work, and you need to move in a different direction." And honestly, Jo was so obedient that, just for the sake of responsibility or obligation or whatever you want to call it, she might have broken it off. But her parents, even early on, were supportive and encouraging. And my parents were of course supportive of her. They still say to this day she is the best thing that ever happened to me.

Despite all the differences between my dad and Chip, Dad knew that he had a good heart, and he saw something in Chip that he knew was right for me.

People say opposites attract, and I think the fact that Chip and I were together for anything beyond a first date proves that point pretty well. But the fact that we *stayed* together goes to something a little deeper. The fact that we were opposites on the surface didn't negate the fact that we were both raised by loving parents, in loving families, and that we both love our families dearly. Our roots were important to both of us, and that one common bond, to me, plays a big role in what has kept us together.

Not that we're perfect or anything. Don't get the wrong idea. There were times when we would fight like cats and dogs. And Jo's tough. But there was just something about her. We'd work through it. Whatever stupid mistake I made—and there was plenty of stuff that set her off—we'd find a way to get through it, and we'd wind up being even closer to each other in the end. Every time.

Jo was more perfect for me than I ever could have imagined. After we'd been dating about a year, I honestly couldn't imagine my life without her. So I decided to do the traditional thing and went and asked Jo's dad for her hand in marriage. Honestly, that was one of the best days of my life. I couldn't have been more nervous, and he was just so supportive. Both of our families were supportive. And as soon as I was over that hurdle, I started planning a way to surprise her and ask her to marry me in a way that she'd never forget.

Chip told me he'd been invited to a private concert, and he asked me if I wanted to go. He was vague about what kind of music it was or what this concert was all about, but I didn't care. I pretty much wanted to go anywhere Chip wanted to take me.

"Okay, great!" he said. "Well, you've got to get really dressed up, and it's in Archer City."

I knew that both of Chip's parents had gone to high school in that sweet little town, which was the setting for Larry McMurtry's famous novel, *The Last Picture Show*, and the movie of the same name starring Cybill Shepherd and Jeff Bridges. The old theater that inspired the book and film was still there, and I knew they had concerts in that venue from time to time, so nothing seemed unusual about Chip's request, even though we would have to drive four hours to get there. I honestly didn't suspect a thing. I was just excited.

We wound up rolling into Archer City at about seven o'clock that night. But instead of pulling up near the theater, Chip pulled into this little shopping center and drove us around to a door in the back.

"Chip, where are you taking me?" I asked.

"Just come on," he said. He was all smiles.

I was thinking, *Well, this must be a super private concert.* He took me into this unmarked hallway, and at first he seemed kind of lost, as if he was trying to figure out where he was going. Then all of a sudden Chip fell down to one knee and sort of wobbled to one side. I thought he was having a heart attack or something.

"Chip? Are you okay?" I said.

I was wearing a peacoat—it was cold out—and when I knelt down, my knee pinned the bottom of my coat to the ground so I couldn't sit back up straight. I had to put my hand against the wall so I could lean and get the jacket out from under me.

Then he looked at me. I realized he was down on one knee on purpose. He got real calm, and he took my hand, and he said, "I want to spend the rest of my life with you." I was in total shock—even more so than I was on my dad's driveway basketball court when Chip first said, "I love you."

"Oh my goodness!" was the only thing I could get out. I was so taken aback, and so happy, but *so* confused.

"Chip," I said, kind of giggling and giddy at the whole thing. "Babe, why are we doing this in a hallway?"

Chip got a funny smile on his face, a smile I'd never seen before, and he said, "Well, knock on the door." We were standing beside an unmarked door in that unmarked hallway, and I could not figure out for the life of me what he was up to. I shook my head and went ahead and knocked—and the door opened.

Behind it stood a man who looked like Geppetto from *Pinocchio*, wearing a leather apron and a magnifying visor on his head.

"Welcome to my jewelry shop," the man said. "You're here to design your ring."

I just about melted. The shopping center was closed, so we had the whole store to ourselves. The jeweler was a man named Billy Holder, who had gone to high school with Chip's dad, and they'd worked this whole thing out in advance. The fact that the selection of the ring tied back to Chip's roots and family history made it all the more special for me.

I couldn't get over the fact that Chip had arranged all of this just for me. *When did he have the time? How did he keep it all a secret?* I wondered. I basically got the chance to sit and sift through Billy's entire inventory of diamonds and settings and pick my engagement ring right there on the spot.

I gave her the pick of any eighty-dollar diamond she wanted.

He's kidding. His budget was actually quite a bit more than eighty dollars. We joked about that, though, because my dad had only had eighty dollars to spend on my mom's engagement ring, and she'd loved it anyway. As soon as they could afford it, she upgraded. But I was so happy, I think I would have been happy with an eighty-dollar ring if that was all Chip could afford.

Sure, if you were the one to pick it out! Even back then, I was smart enough to know you were real opinionated. If I'd gone and picked out the ring myself, I could literally have seen you going, "Hey, I really do love you, and you and me are gonna work out fine, but there's no way that's the ring I'm gonna wear."

Oh, and just to clarify about my answer to Chip—at some point after saying, "Oh my goodness," I did say yes.

Chip said his mom had loaned him some money, so I was able to get something really special. We didn't have tens of thousands of dollars to spend, and thankfully we weren't buying diamonds in Beverly Hills. I was able to pick out a nice round diamond and a beautiful, antique-looking platinum setting.

I had a blast sitting there with Billy, designing the perfect ring. Chip just sat there, patiently observing every second of it. After we finished designing, Billy said he would need some time to work on the ring, so he gave me a substitute to wear for the time being, just for fun. It was a great big, gaudy fake diamond that he'd put together so I would have something to show off to my friends and family.

"Your parents are gonna go crazy wondering how much money you spent on this!" Billy said to Chip with a laugh.

There was no private concert that night, but Chip did have more in store for me. From Billy's shop we drove over to this cute little Archer City hotel for dinner. My parents, my little sister, Chip's parents, and his sister were all there waiting to celebrate our engagement with us.

There were all sorts of hugs and tears of joy that made that night the most perfect night ever, and of course they were all taken aback by the size of my "diamond." It's funny to me that, even way back then, they all seemed to realize that a flashy ring just wasn't my style. They expected to see me wearing something a little subtler, a little smaller, a little more classic maybe. But we strung them along for a good long while, and we all had a good laugh when Chip finally revealed that the ring was fake.

Twelve years later, we had the opportunity to invite Billy Holder out to the farm for our anniversary party. Chip surprised me that night with a twelve-year anniversary strand of pearls that Billy hand-delivered to me, and we had the cameras there to capture the whole moment. It aired as part of our third season. But what the cameras didn't show was the moment when we went back to the farm and found Billy sitting on my front porch holding a selection of diamonds on a black velvet tray. "Chip wants you to upgrade," he said to me.

"My engagement ring?" I said.

"Yes! He knows you love the setting, but he wants you to be able to pick out a better diamond like your mom did."

That first diamond was beautiful, but it was simple in nature. It was all we could afford back then, but at this point I wanted to do something nicer. Something bigger. So I'd told Billy to bring some options so we could replace it with something else. I thought of it as an investment of sorts, and I wanted it to be perfect.

So Billy showed me all of these beautiful diamonds and told me I could have my pick. That's supposed to be every girl's dream, right? But I looked him in the eye, and I said, "I'm sorry, but no. This is the original diamond I picked, and it's perfect just the way it is."

It wasn't a "perfect" diamond, but it was perfect for me. I felt bad that Billy wasn't going to make the big sale he was hoping for that day, but I don't ever want to replace that diamond *or* that ring. To me, my ring is part of our story.

If I looked down at my hand and saw a more expensive diamond in that setting, it somehow wouldn't fit. I would know that we couldn't have afforded that diamond back when we first got engaged. The story wouldn't add up.

But this ring, with this diamond, the one I wear every day—this ring *fits*. When I look at it, I remember picking out that very diamond on the night of our engagement and looking at it through the little magnifier. I think about the look on Chip's face when he looked up at me in that hallway. And inevitably, I can't stop myself from thinking of where it led us six months later: our wedding.

THREE

SOMETHING OLD, SOMETHING NEW

S ometimes I think, *If I were to do my wedding today, I would do things differently.* With everything I've learned, the places I've gone, the design ideas I've seen, I would want to include all sorts of details that I never could have even imagined back then.

But then I flip open our wedding album and see the smiling faces of the people we love all gathered in that place where we chose to celebrate our special day together, and just as with my engagement ring, any desire for something different or fancier melts away. Our wedding was perfect just the way it was. Everything we cared about was exactly the way we wanted. When I look back, I realize I wouldn't change a single thing.

Chip and I got married here in Waco on May 31, 2003, at the Earle Harrison House, a historic mansion that looks an awful lot like the place where we had our first date—a stately manor with grand pillars and a gorgeous garden. We actually chose the location primarily because of its parklike setting. We wanted an outdoor wedding, and the gardens there were filled with roses.

The place was completely covered in flowers climbing high on grand arbors that our guests would walk under. The setting was so beautiful just the way it was. I didn't need much of a budget for flowers. I loved magnolias even back then, before the shop came along, so we cut individual magnolia leaves for our guests to use as fans.

My parents had sat us down shortly after we announced our engagement and made us an offer. They'd been married on the steps of a courthouse, and with that in mind they'd said they were going to give us a certain amount of money as an up-front wedding gift. We could use that money for whatever we wanted—to throw a nicer wedding than we could afford on our own (although *anything* would have been more than we could afford on our own at that point) or to throw a simple wedding and use that money on a down payment for a home or a honeymoon or whatever we chose.

Chip and I decided that we would use the money for the wedding. Since our plan was to move into one of his soon-to-be-vacated student rental houses on Third Street for the summer, we didn't need extra for a down payment. And Chip's parents had been kind enough to take care of the honeymoon, so we were set.

I had no desire for a high-priced designer dress, so I went out shopping with my mom and found one off the rack for around five hundred dollars. Just a simple, white, Cinderella-looking dress with a lace-up back—narrow at the waist and then flowing out through the skirt. Chip and his groomsmen wore rented tuxedos from the mall. We weren't interested in capturing the latest trends or trying to impress anybody. We just wanted it to be beautiful, and the best way I knew to do that was to stick to a classic, timeless look, so black-and-white attire with red roses was the palette we chose. Plus, we knew all of those beautiful white roses in the Harrison House gardens would give us the perfect backdrop we dreamed of.

The day before the wedding, we went over to the property for the rehearsal and I just about died: the estate had pruned all of the roses. They were gone—every last one of them! There was nothing there but empty stems. The arbors, the arch over the altar, everything was just leaves and thorns.

Sadly, it just happened to be the time of year to prune the roses. It was a professionally kept garden, like an arboretum, and the time had come. I mean, I *think* they could have waited an extra day or two know-ing they had a wedding that weekend, but it was too late to argue. In a last-minute attempt to save the scene, we scrambled to our parents to ask for a flower budget. We bought hundreds and hundreds of white roses and stuck them in bunches all over the arbors and barren bushes, doing our best to fill in a million holes and make it look like the real roses were still there.

When I look at pictures now, it may be obvious that those roses had been stuck in by hand, but that wasn't the point. It was honestly almost *better* that all of our closest friends and family had come together at the last minute and tried to turn this venue back into the place we'd been dreaming about.

It really was perfect—perfect for *us*—and part of the reason for that is we broke tradition in some ways. For example, Chip insisted that his dog, Shiner, be in the wedding. We haven't mentioned Chip's dog yet, but that mutt was Chip's best friend. I still swear to this day that he loved that dog more than he loved me. My bridesmaids weren't crazy about the idea of Shiner being a member of the wedding party, but Chip wouldn't budge. Heck, Shiner would've been Chip's best man if he could've stood at the end of that aisle and held those rings. But we compromised and set him up under a gorgeous oak tree so he could be comfortable in the shade as he watched his old man get married.

My dad and I arrived at the ceremony by horse-drawn carriage. A trumpeter played us in. We had a little string quartet and a beautiful couple who sang during the ceremony. All of our closest friends were there. It was a day we'll never forget.

I still look back at it as one of the best days of my life. A lot of my friends and her friends met for the first time at this wedding, because we were literally from different universes. But they were all so impor-tant to us, and I just remember that all my buddies were like, "She has got the sweetest friends!"

All these people kind of came together and became buddies. It was great. And there were some funny coincidences too. Jo had twins in her wedding party, and I had twins in mine. I mean, what are the chances of that?

Chip's dad was his best man. My sisters were my maid and matron of honor. The fact that our friends got along so well and that we both put family first were just more signs to me that Chip and I weren't all that different where it counted. There were a lot of similarities between us, and that day seemed to be filled with affirmations of just how much we truly belonged together.

The wedding seemed to have a ripple effect too. My sister Mary Kay brought this guy to the wedding that she'd only been on a few dates with. His name was David. Well, she caught the bouquet, he caught the garter, and they wound up getting married too. How's that for a story?

Chip and I started our honeymoon off in New York City, where I had done my internship. One of my favorite things to do when I lived alone in New York was just walk its streets. There are fascinating landmarks around every corner, people of every culture and background and style you could ever imagine, and so many interesting shops and restaurants. No matter how many times you walked those streets, you would always, always find something new.

One of the most surprising finds to me were the little individual shops and boutiques, whether they were clothing stores or home furnishing stores or gift shops. It was almost as if the owners of those little individual shops had to work extra hard to make sure their businesses could compete with the big chains and expensive stores all over town—and the results were incredible.

There always seemed to be a candle burning, filling those shops with the delicious scents. It wasn't unusual to see fresh flowers on the counter next to the cash register or for the shopkeeper to offer you a cup of coffee or tea while you browsed. There was something just wonderfully inviting and warm about those places that made me feel very connected in a city that could sometimes feel big and overwhelming.

I loved taking Chip to that great big city and showing him a side of me he hadn't seen before. We acted like rich kids and stayed in a suite at the Drake Hotel, a high-end, first-class place on Park Avenue that had once played host to celebrities like Frank Sinatra and Lillian Gish. But that was just the starting point for our adventure.

We set aside a full two weeks for our honeymoon, and other than those couple of nights at the Drake, we made no plans whatsoever. We decided to rent a little car and just go wherever the day took us. We headed upstate and marveled as the massive city gave way so quickly to hills and rivers and fields full of flowers. Before long the tallest buildings around were the silos on old-fashioned farms that dotted the landscape.

Chip and I both had an affection for farms and old barns and silos, and we decided it would be fun to go explore. If we saw an abandoned barn, all gray and weathered and tipping over in some empty field, we'd stop and go walk around it, even duck inside just to see what was there. Occasionally we'd find old bottles and farm equipment, and I always wondered why someone had just up and abandoned them there for all those years.

The thing I found interesting was just how beautiful everything looked. The rust, the age, the weathering—maybe it was just because we were in love, but everything we saw in those old abandoned barns, both inside and out, seemed to capture and reflect the beauty of the land and the air and the early summer scents in that beautiful corner of the world. Even the dust in those old barns seemed to rise up on purpose, helping to illuminate those old forgotten spaces with streams of sunlight that crept through the cracks in the wood.

We didn't have Google Maps in 2003, so we spent that honeymoon road trip following our intuition and heeding the attraction of little signs on the side of the road: "Antiques" or "Bed & Breakfast" or "Pick-Ur-Own!" We agreed that we would drive until we were both dead tired and then find someplace to lay our heads wherever we happened to wind up.

On the first night we ran into this place called the Mohonk Mountain House. We'd been driving along the cliffs of the Hudson River, and then all of a sudden this hotel made of stone rose up in front of our eyes. It looked just like some sort of medieval castle.

It was late, and we were exhausted from all of our exploring, and we both thought we'd died or something. "Is this place for real? Or did we just drive off that cliff to get here?" It was so weird just to cruise into some driveway and have no idea what to expect and then find a place like that.

We wandered into the lobby half expecting it to be our final resting place.

The good news is we weren't dead, and when we told the nice people at the front desk that we were on our honeymoon, they put us up in a gorgeous penthouse suite for the price of a regular room.

People wound up giving us deals like that almost everywhere we went on that trip. It was incredible. And thank goodness, because we were already low on funds.

From there, we decided to continue up into New England, meandering across the Berkshires in western Massachusetts, cutting through the country roads of southern New Hampshire, and heading north to explore as much of the crashing Atlantic on the rocky Maine coast as we could. We stayed off the interstates and took back roads as much as possible, stopping at antiques stores and mom-and-pop shops and cute old barns and farmhouses—whatever caught our eye. One night we stayed in the dreamiest bed-and-breakfast right on a farm, where we ate fresh eggs and a home-cooked meal in the morning. Both of us agreed, "What could be better than that?"

Before I met Chip, I was basically a city girl—or maybe a suburban girl. As a kid I lived in a typical cookie-cutter neighborhood in Wichita, Kansas. We lived there until I was twelve, while my dad kind of worked his way up the corporate ladder for Firestone. But as a small child I would often go visit my friend's farm. She had silos that we would play in—I thought that was the coolest thing.

My friend hated living out on that farm. She wanted to come play at my house so she could be in a neighborhood, riding bikes with all my friends. But I liked going to her house because it *was* a farm. We would pretend we were these farm girls that wore aprons, and we'd come up with stories like, "Let's pretend that Bobby got stuck in the silo." We played so much make-believe at that farm that I feel as though farm living was a part of my past, even though it really wasn't. Driving through the beautiful farmlands along the back roads of New York brought back the memories of my time spent there.

The grass is always greener, right? We were both brought up in these sort of cookie-cutter neighborhoods, but in my case, I loved going to my granddad's ranch. That was definitely where I got the cowboy in my personality. My granddad J. B. was a bona fide cowboy. He was like the Marlboro man, literally—smoked cigarettes, tall, lean, great-looking dude, always had this gorgeous cowboy hat on, wore long-sleeved shirts and long pants every day of his life, even when it was a hundred degrees outside. He was just one of these iconic characters. I still to this day think of him as the hero of all heroes, the legend of all legends.

I don't mean to overstate that, because my dad was a huge hero to me too. He was the one who was there, who loved us, who was at every ball game, and my granddad wasn't the doting, overtly loving kind of guy. But he was kind of the patriarch of the family, and spending time with him on that ranch made a big impact on my life.

I may have grown up in the suburbs, like most kids did, but I've always felt like J. B. and I had a lot in common. And I've always felt like I was born a hundred years too late.

For either of us to romanticize farm life was probably a silly thing to do. It's a lot of work. For my friend, living on a farm just meant she had a whole lot of chores to do. But no matter how much I heard her complain, I still thought, *That's what I want someday.* So having that little taste of farm life on our honeymoon sure felt right to both of us.

Days later, somewhere along the woodsy coast of Maine, at around eleven o'clock at night, we had another memorable moment. We were tooling around a corner when Chip slammed on the brakes, squealing to a dead stop. He and I both stared out through the windshield and said, "What in the world is that?!"

Luckily we weren't in a hurry and weren't driving too fast, because right in front of us was this big, awkward-looking moose standing right in the middle of the road. Neither one of us had ever seen one in person, and we just could not believe how big this thing was. It was like a dream come true for me to come across an animal like that in the wild.

Once I realized what it was, I was like, "What should we do? I feel like we should do something!" But Jo said, "Let the poor thing go," so I did. We watched that majestic beast wander off into the woods and disappear in the darkness just as fast as he'd shown up in our headlights.

I feel like the moose was our final big find of that trip. We were both tired, and after seeing something that magnificent, we decided it was time to head home. We took a different route down through Boston and realized as we drove through the city that we were basically out of money.

We had nothing left. We stayed on the interstates after that and made it back to New York with as few stops as possible, arriving just in time to fly back home.

Jo's idea of being "broke" was when she had, like, $1,000 left in the bank. But "broke" for me meant actually broke. I wasn't much for bank accounts or credit cards back then. So once we got back to Waco, we literally had no money left for a hotel room or anything. We had no choice but to go straight to the vacated rental house we were planning to move into.

The students had just moved out of it while we were on our honeymoon, and it was nighttime when we got back home, so we didn't have a chance to get in and inspect it or clean the place or anything like that. We just drove in from the airport and pulled up in front of that little yellow house on Third Street, at the end of this dreamy honeymoon of a lifetime—

And Chip carried me over the threshold. Right into a nightmare.

FOUR

THE HONEYMOON'S OVER

The rental houses on Third Street that Chip owned when we got married were really small, and not the most attractive homes. I wouldn't have chosen to live in any one of them if I could avoid it. Thankfully, though, the nicest one of the bunch happened to open up at the end of the spring semester, and Chip hadn't put any summer renters into it yet. It was a yellow ranch-style with a nice white porch on the front and a pair of huge magnolia trees in the yard, and it was bigger than the rest—maybe twelve hundred square feet or so. It was just pretty enough that I was excited to live there and fix it up—to make it feel like our very own home.

Chip and I were both exhausted when we finally pulled up in front of that house, but we were still riding the glow of our honeymoon, and I was so excited as he carried me over the threshold—until the smell nearly knocked us over.

"Oh my word," I said, pinching my nose and trying to hold my breath so I wouldn't gag. "What is that?"

Chip flicked the light switch, and the light didn't come on. He flicked it up and down a few times, then felt his way forward in the darkness and tried another switch.

"The electricity's off," he said. "The girls must've had it shut off when they moved out."

"Didn't you transfer it back into your name?" I asked.

"I guess not. I'm sorry, babe," Chip said.

"Chip, *what* is that *smell*?"

It was the middle of June in Waco, Texas. The temperature had been up over a hundred degrees for days on end, and the humidity was stifling, amplifying whatever that rotten smell was coming from the kitchen. Chip always carries a knife and a flashlight, and it sure came in handy that night. Chip made his way back there and found that the fridge still had a bunch of food left in it, including a bunch of ground beef that had just sat there rotting since whenever the electricity went out.

The food was literally just smoldering in this hundred-degree house. So we went from living in a swanky hotel room on Park Avenue in New York City to this disgusting, humid stink of a place that felt more like the site of a crime scene than a home at this point. Honestly, I hadn't thought it through very well. But it was late, and we were tired, and I just focused on making the most of this awful situation.

So we opened some windows and brought our bags in, and I told Jo we'd just tough it out and sleep on the floor and clean it all up in the morning. That's when she started crying.

I lay down on the floor thinking, *Is this what my life is going to look like now that I married Chip? Is this my new normal?*

That's when another smell hit me. It was in the carpet.

"Chip, did those girls have a dog here?" I asked.

"They had a couple of dogs," he answered. "Why?"

You could smell it. In the carpet. It was nasty. I was just lying there with my head next to some old dog urine stain that had been heated by the Texas summer heat.

It was like microwaved dog pee.

It was. It was awful. It was three in the morning. And I finally said, "Chip, I'm not sleeping in this house."

We were broke. We couldn't go to a hotel. There was no way we were gonna go knock on one of our parents' doors at that time of night.

That's when I got an idea. We happened to have Chip's parents' old RV parked in a vacant lot a few blocks down. We had some of our things in there and had been using it basically as a storage unit until we moved in. "Let's get in the RV. We'll go find somewhere to plug it in, and we'll have AC," I said.

As we stepped outside, the skies opened up. It started pouring rain. When we finally got into the RV, soaking wet, we pulled down the road a ways and Chip said, "I know where we can go." It was raining so hard we could barely see through the windshield, and all of a sudden Chip turned the RV into a cemetery.

"Why are you pulling in to a cemetery?" I asked him.

"We're not going to the cemetery," Chip said. "It's just *next to* a cemetery. There's an RV park back here."

"Are you kidding me? Could this get any worse?"

"Oh, quit it. You're going to love it once I get this AC fired up."

Chip decided to go flying through the median between two rows of RV parking, not realizing it was set up like a culvert for drainage and rain runoff. That RV bounced so hard that, had it not been for our seat belts, we would've both been catapulted through the roof of that vehicle.

"What was that?!"

"I don't know," Chip said.

I tried to put it in reverse, and then forward, and then reverse again, and the thing just wouldn't move. I hopped out to take a look and couldn't believe it. There was a movie a few years ago where the main character gets his RV caught on this fulcrum and it's sitting there teetering with both sets of wheels up in the air. Well, we sort of did the opposite. We went across this valley, and because the RV was so long, the butt end of it got stuck on the little hill behind us, and the front end got stuck on the little hill in front of us, and the wheels were just sort of hanging there in between. I crawled back into the RV soaking wet and gave Jo the bad news.

We had no place to go, no place to plug in so we could run the AC; it was pouring rain so we couldn't really walk anywhere to get help. And at that point I was just done. We wound up toughing it out and spending the first night after our honeymoon in a hot, old RV packed full of our belongings, suspended between two bumps in the road.

The next morning, someone from the RV park spotted us and was kind enough to call a tow truck. The first truck they sent wasn't big enough, so they had to call in a semi tow truck. One of the big ones. We were freaking out, of course, 'cause we were flat broke. (Are you starting to pick up on a theme here? We stayed flat broke a lot of the time early on.) We didn't know how we were going to pay this guy. But then our very last little honeymooner's miracle came through. That truck driver said, "Well, guys, it looks like the honeymoon is over. This one's on us."

This was just the way things were with Chip. He was always going out on a limb, but God always had a way of looking out for him. Actually, God seemed to always be out on that limb with him, taking care of him. We should have been more careful not to spend every last dollar on our honeymoon. But that favor from that sweet man made us feel as if maybe some things were just meant to be.

By the light of day, we went back to the yellow house full of hot stink, and I made up my mind right then and there to make the best of it. I pulled myself together and rolled up my sleeves (as people say), and I said to Chip, "Okay. Let's do this."

What else could I do? This was our home now. We didn't have any other options. I covered my nose and mouth and started cleaning. Once the two of us got the worst of it out, Chip went off and took care of some business. There were rent checks in from his other houses that needed to be cashed, and as soon as we had a few dollars in hand, we hit the hardware store.

I had never done anything design-related at that point, but there was something very liberating about starting from scratch. We knew every room needed to be painted, all the carpet needed to come out, and all the hardwood floors needed to be refinished. And Chip gave me free rein to make that home whatever I wanted to make it.

To be honest, I didn't know what I wanted to make it, so I started with one basic idea: "I have, like, six favorite colors, so I'm going to paint every room one of those colors."

Once I got going, I decided that using different colors in every room wasn't enough for me. I wanted to make every room a different *theme*. I went with a nautical theme in the front room and decorated with a bunch of cheap sailboats and netting that I bought at a hobby store. The kitchen was French-inspired, so it was mustard yellow. Our bedroom was hotel-inspired—all white. The back room was Chip-inspired, so it was cedar and horns and cowhides. Every room was completely different.

We did every part of this renovation together with our bare hands. Chip restored all of the wood floors, all the tile work—everything. I was learning as we went, but I definitely did my part.

That house was gorgeous. Jo did an awesome job helping fix it up, and her ideas were great. There was a moment in the kitchen when I smarted off, though. I don't even remember what I said, to be honest, but Jo got real mad and started yelling. She was carrying this five-gallon bucket of primer. She slammed it down on the ground to make a point, and it splashed right back up in her face. It was dripping off her eyelashes and her nose.

Whenever something like that happened in my family, we'd all just laugh, you know? So I laughed, even though she was mad at me, and that made her even angrier. She started yelling again with the primer dripping all over, and I just had this moment where I looked at her and everything seemed to be going in slow motion and I thought, *I love this woman. She is tough! Oh, this is gonna work.*

That was our first real "fight," and even now we both agree it was our biggest. Chip had smarted off about something, so my blood was already boiling, but when I slammed that bucket down, Chip says I became a ninja—the kind you don't want to mess with. Yet he *still* laughed, against his better judgment. We joke about it now, like, "Well, I'm mad, but I'm not primer-in-the-face mad."

It would take us a few months to get everything in livable condition in that house, even though we were living there full-time. Looking back, I don't know how we did it, but I guess you have a lot more time and energy before there are kids in the picture. We were newlyweds. We had our whole lives ahead of us. And despite the rough start, we were still riding the excitement of our honeymoon and feeding off of that energy we seemed to have whenever we were together, which was basically all the time.

Chip never said no to any of my ideas. He was 100 percent on board for my various theme rooms. He spoiled me in that way. But it was more than that. Chip supported everything I wanted to do. He even supported my dreams. The two of us would dream together all the time, just lying in bed at night, imagining where we could go in life, talking about things we always wanted to do or see or accomplish.

Until I left home and went to do my internship in New York City, I honestly didn't know what I wanted to do. At some point in my teen years, I told my father that I wanted to take over his Firestone shop when he retired. I thought that was the right thing to do. I thought it would make him proud, as if I were the son he'd never had who would step into his shoes and carry on the successful business he'd created.

Then I went to Baylor and got interested in broadcast journalism. I loved the storytelling and the editing process, and I managed to get two years' worth of internships under my belt at our local CBS station, KWTX. Everyone said that if you wanted to make it in TV news you had to go to New York City to do it, so I went out on a limb and applied to the *Today* show, *Good Morning America*, and *48 Hours*. Those shows didn't have internship affiliations with Baylor at the time, so it was a long shot to say the least. I just went and did it on my own out of blind, naive ambition, I guess.

I had lived a pretty sheltered life up until then, so when *48 Hours* selected me, I was worried my parents might fight it. How could they let their little girl go to the big city by herself? But I was wrong. My protective parents not only supported my ambition, they paid for my apartment for those six months—a good thing, too, because it was fifteen hundred dollars a month for a room in a shared apartment with two other people!

As amazing as it was to live on West 57th Street and to work under a man as esteemed as Dan Rather, I quickly fell out of love with the news business while working that job. My job as an intern was to read the papers to find salacious stories, cold cases, or horrible crime stories to pitch to the senior editors. It was heavy.

While I fell out of love with TV news, I did fall in love with New York City. It was more than just wandering in and out of those lovely boutiques that I mentioned before. I was pretty homesick during those six months, and I especially missed my mother. So it was eye-opening and beautiful to see so many people in that big city who looked like my mom and me. It seemed that everywhere I looked there was a woman walking down the street who reminded me of her. It was so unlike growing up in Kansas and Texas. New York is where I finally began to appreciate all of the different cultures and truly began to fall in love with my Korean heritage.

It's difficult to put into words, but there was something about that experience that helped me find myself. I would go home every night and write about my experiences—what I'd seen, what I'd done, and sometimes just about whatever I was thinking or feeling. And as I did that, something shifted in me. I started owning who I am, realizing that I was unique and that God had a unique purpose for me. I'd spent my whole life worrying about what people thought about me or whether I was good enough or thinking about what I *should* be doing instead of really digging down to find out what I *wanted* to do.

I had always been a religious person. I was brought up in the church, and my parents were very committed to getting the family there every Sunday without fail. So from the age of five to about twenty, religion to me was a matter of "you do this, and you don't do that, and you do your best to walk the straight line."

I was good at that. I'm good at following the rules—most of the time. But once I was on my own in New York, my faith became something very personal. It was no longer about what my parents knew or what my pastor knew. I came to think of God as more of a gracious friend who was accompanying me on this journey, a friend who wanted to carry my burdens and speak into my life and shape me into who I really was and who I would become.

When I came back to Waco, I had a very different perspective. I went back to work at my father's Firestone shop knowing that I didn't want to do broadcast journalism, but also doubting whether or not I wanted to take over the tire business. I spent a good part of my days in that back office daydreaming and sketching ideas out on a yellow steno pad.

I wasn't sure I wanted to run my dad's business, but I definitely liked the idea of owning my own business. I thought about what kind of business I'd like to own—a spa, a bakery, a home store. Whatever I chose, I wanted it to be as beautiful and welcoming as those boutiques in New York.

I drew pictures of what the shops might look like. I designed logos. I never shared those ideas with anybody, and there were times when I thought I was just being foolish. In fact, I started to think about my degree and the fact that I'd worked at one of the top evening news programs in all of television, and I wondered if maybe I'd given up on TV news too soon. I wondered if maybe I should go back to New York and go for it. I was actually in the middle of pulling up all the old contacts I'd made during my internship on the very day I met Chip at the tire shop.

And so I stayed in Waco, and my life took a sharp turn down a path I never could've imagined.

We'd only been living in the yellow house for about a month when I flipped open that yellow pad and showed Chip some of my ideas. Remodeling and redecorating that house had filled me with all sorts of new inspiration, so I showed him the sketches and plans I had made for a little home décor shop. I told him I wanted to apply everything I'd learned from this house and my days wandering around Manhattan to a business idea I'd been playing around with.

"Someday," I said.

"Why not right now?" Chip replied.

"What do you mean?"

"Go drive around and find a building you like, and let's do it. We'll fix it up just like we're fixing up this house, and you can open your business right now."

"Are you serious?"

"Of course I'm serious! Go find a building and let's do it! Why not?"

Chip had this way of turning far-off dreams into something that seemed real and achievable in an instant. He filled me up with a confidence I'd never known. He made me believe I could actually do it.

So I did.

I drove around Waco with new eyes, searching around every corner and strip mall for something that I could turn into my vision. One day, I spotted this little building on Bosque (pronounced BOSS-key) Boulevard. It was sunburnt orange—a bit like Chip on our first date— and it was all boarded up, but it looked more like a little house than a cookie-cutter, strip-mall type of business. It backed up to a residential neighborhood, it had its own little parking lot, and it was right next door to a church. There was something cute and quirky about the place that just caught my eye.

It wasn't for sale. It basically looked abandoned. But I took a picture on my phone and sent it to Chip.

"I love this building!" I told him.

His response was, "Jo, that thing is ugly."

"But I love all the windows, and I can imagine these pretty displays . . ."

I've picked some dumps, some buildings that weren't pretty, either. But this place seemed like it was on the wrong side of town for a retail location. It looked more like a place that you'd turn into a little gas station or a used car lot or something.

Chip didn't feel good about it, but he did some research anyway and found out the property was owned by a woman named Maebelle, who was probably in her seventies at the time. We reached out to her, and she agreed to meet us at the building. She told us the whole history of the place. Her son had been renovating it for years, but he had gotten very sick and had never been able to finish. She'd received a couple of offers on the property, but she just wasn't ready to part with it yet—especially since those bidders wanted to turn it into a used car lot or something else she didn't want to see in the neighborhood. She and her son had been looking to open a tuxedo shop, and she was hoping for something along those lines.

We had a good talk with Maebelle, and she loved the idea that I'd be opening a shop I would run myself, that I had no interest in tearing down that little building her son had worked on for so long. Before we left, we told her we'd like to make an offer too, and she said that when the time came she would rather sell it to us than to the other folks.

So we got all excited. Thinking back, maybe we got excited a little too quickly. Because we'd never thought through exactly how we'd finance the place.

I had a line of credit that worked well for flipping houses. It was a short-term thing. But I didn't have the credit needed to do a long-term commercial purchase like that. Even though this was gonna be Jo's business, it made sense to both of us that it should be in both our names.

I had a tiny bit of savings tucked away that I decided I could use for a down payment. I'd never thought I would touch that money, but Chip inspired me to want to do something more with it than just let it sit in the bank earning next to nothing in interest. I also knew that if I filled out a loan application, I'd still be able to show the income I'd been making at my dad's shop. I might even be able to qualify for some kind of small-business loan available to women. We decided to go for it and were excited to hear about some financing options Chip hadn't used before.

The bottom line was that I loved Jo, she loved me, and we loved being together. Working together energized us—it just worked out best. And no matter what it took, I was going to make this little shop work for her. When she shared that little yellow notepad of sketches with me, I knew this was like Jo sharing her diary or something. These were her innermost thoughts and dreams. I couldn't help but push her toward them. And the quicker, I thought, the better. No time to chicken out. Just like our first date.

After doing all the paperwork and scraping together as much as I could, I offered Maebelle $45,000 for her property. And she said, "Oh my. I've already had two offers for considerably more than that." She had thought we would come closer to those other offers, and she'd been sure she'd pick us over them, even if we came in a little under, simply because she liked us. But $45,000 was just too low.

"I am so sorry. I thought you guys were going to be a little closer," she said.

"I am so sorry if I offended you, Maebelle. That's just what I have," I said.

"Well, if you could come up with more, call me," she replied. "If not, I'm going to have to move on with these other people."

I knew we couldn't come up with more. Putting together the financing on that $45,000 was a stretch as it was. That was that.

I was really sad about it, of course. I'd managed to get all excited imagining the possibilities for what I could do in that location. I'd envisioned that shop from top to bottom. I swear I could smell the candles burning inside and see the looks on my customers' faces when they found that perfectly unique item that would fit in that perfect spot in their home.

I wasn't ready to give up. I knew we could probably find another location somewhere. But it was very hard to let go of the store I'd envisioned in that quirky old building on Bosque.

So that night and just about every night after that, I prayed: "Lord, that's the building that spoke to me. And if it's meant to be, please make it come back around."

FIVE

OPENING UP

Sometimes the thing we're dreaming of doesn't work out. But Chip and I weren't going to give up on the idea of opening my shop just because the building I fell in love with seemed to slip through our fingers. So we kept on looking for other buildings. We searched and searched, but nothing we found had the character and charm of that little spot on Bosque.

I was starting to lose hope when, a few weeks into our renewed search, my prayers were suddenly answered. Maebelle called me on my cell phone: "Joanna, I've been praying about it, and I do not know why, but I feel very strongly that God is saying I need to sell this building to you for $45,000."

I could hardly believe it. God made it so evident that this was meant to be. I was about to open my very own business!

Some friends and family members tried to talk me out of doing this. They felt it was just too big of a risk to take because I had no experience running a business of my own, no training in retail sales or marketing. I had never owned property before. And I knew next to nothing about home décor or design. Truly, the only home decorating I'd ever done was in the house where we were currently living, and that had just been one big experiment for me.

But Chip did what Chip does and made all those facts, all that logic, seem irrelevant. He really did. He believed I could do it, and he was confident that what I didn't know, I could learn.

I think part of what originally drew me to TV journalism was that I was a curious observer of other people. I may have been the quiet girl, but I was always the one who watched how things worked and took everything in. I'd told Chip all about how things worked in those shops in New York. Time spent by shoppers in those little boutiques was a sensory experience, and the store owners made sure of it. Women, especially, notice these kinds of details: the sweet smell of a candle burning, the color of a fresh bouquet of flowers next to the register, the music softly playing in the background, the allure of an interesting display—all of those things I'd mentioned earlier. As a shopper and a careful observer, I was able to appreciate the creative process that went into each little table and window installation.

In that sense, I wanted to create a store that was an experience, not just a collection of things for people to buy. I wanted to design it with intention and be sure I set things up to catch the eye of my shoppers. I also wanted to make sure my displays were practical and inspired my visitors to know that they, too, could set up their homes like this. My goal was to make design relatable, to make it attainable.

We took some time renovating that little houselike shop while I finished up our remodeling at home, and in the process I started collecting inventory. I bought inexpensive merchandise at the Dallas Market Center, an incredible wholesale marketplace filled with items sourced from all over the world. I hit garage sales and flea markets, too, and found old mirrors and furniture and knickknacks that I could fix up or distress to make them more appealing while adding some value to them.

At one point I found a large brown wicker sleigh for five bucks. I couldn't believe how cheap it was. I thought to myself, *If I dress this thing up a bit, I could sell it for twenty-five dollars.* Off to the local craft store I went. I found a fake ivy garland to wrap all around the sleigh and some battery-operated Christmas lights that I tucked into the ivy. I was so proud of the way it turned out that I thought maybe I could sell it before the shop even opened and get a taste for how this would all work. So I talked my father into putting it in his waiting area at Firestone with a price tag on it.

But a week went by, and I noticed the sleigh was still there. The second week, I called my dad. "Yes, JoJo, it's still here. But don't worry. It will sell." The third week went by, and I told my dad that if it didn't sell, I would just come pick it up and get it out of his way. At that point I felt deflated. I questioned more than ever if running a store was what I was supposed to be doing. But I went in toward the end of that third week, and my father handed me an envelope with twenty-five dollars in it. "I told you it would sell," he said. "Now go buy something for twenty dollars and see if you can sell it for fifty bucks. This is how retail works, JoJo."

Selling that sleigh made me feel like I could do this design thing despite the odds—and my lack of experience. But the more I shopped for bargains that I could turn around for profit, the harder it was to choose between what I wanted to sell and what I wanted to use to finish turning our house into a home over on Third Street.

It took nearly eight months to get it to a point where that yellow house finally felt finished. I was so happy to be done, to be free of the dust and debris and tools everywhere, and to finally get the place neatened up and livable. I don't like a lot of clutter. I like a clean house. If my house is too messy, I just can't think straight. And remodeling a house is messy by definition. So nearly eight months after being carried into a house full of rotten meat and dog urine, I was thrilled to finally have a place where we could be comfortable. I was proud of what we'd done too. I hoped we'd live there for a long time, and I was ready to focus all of my energies on the shop.

Then Chip came home one afternoon and said, "Hey, Jo, I bought a new house."

"Oh," I said. "To rent out?"

"Well, eventually, yeah. We're gonna be able to rent this house out now, because we fixed it up. It's ready to go. So let's move down to this next house a few doors down and we'll fix that one up, too, as nice as we made this one. We'll be able to make better rent on everything if we make 'em all look this good."

As I rode down the street with him to see what he'd bought, I was in shock when he pulled up in front of this tiny white box of a house. I mean *tiny*—maybe eight hundred square feet. There was no cute front porch. The yard—front and back—was all weeds and overgrown bushes. When he opened the front door on that cabin-size house, I could see it hadn't been touched in thirty years.

She cried. Again. That was sort of her thing during year one. If we ever write a marriage book, chapter 1 will be called, "She cried."

Chip assured me this was the right thing to do. This was how we were going to get ahead and make real money. He tried to remind me of the fun I'd had fixing up the yellow house, and I had to admit that some parts of it had been fun. I'd loved coming up with the themes for the rooms, and picking out all the colors and textures, and learning how to do the work myself. But the yellow house wasn't just some house to me after doing all of that work. It was *my* house. It was our *home*.

But Chip never saw it like that. He really never got attached to anything that didn't have a heartbeat. These houses, they were just inventory to him. He liked messing with them, but he certainly didn't want to live in any of them forever.

Even though he didn't understand why I was upset, he was smart enough to just leave me alone for a little while. I went back home and sat on the porch and thought, *How can we just rent this house out to college kids? My house.* We'd only been in there eight months. Then I got to thinking about how much work it had been, and the idea of starting from scratch again seemed daunting, especially with everything I was trying to do to get the shop opened up. I cried it out until I reached a point where I realized there was nothing much I could do about it. *He's already bought it, so we're kind of in this now. No one is going to rent that little white house out in the condition it's in.*

One thing I learned there on that beautiful front porch was if I wanted to be successful, if I wanted to do important work one day, I would have to increase my capacity. I had to learn to manage disappointment. I needed to learn how to make the most out of those "opportunities" Chip seemed to keep finding.

So I told Chip okay. We rented our house out that very week to some college students and moved ourselves down the block. We started renovating again. And because this house was half the size and I was already actively out there looking for inventory for the shop, it didn't take nearly as long to get everything finished.

We did suffer a few setbacks, like the time Chip decided to surprise me by using maroon grout on the white tile in the kitchen. He could tell I didn't like it the moment I walked in the room, and he wound up ripping it all out and doing it all over again. I'm not sure why I had such clear ideas about what I liked and didn't like, but I did. And the funny thing is that after a couple of months, once I had put my stamp on it, I was as much in love with that little house as I had been with the yellow one.

She jokes to this day, "I liked that house because I could vacuum the whole place without ever unplugging the cord."

I could plug into one outlet and vacuum every room! I loved that. It's true.

Back at my shop, the one thing I was having a hard time designing was a sign for the front of the building.

Chip and I had decided together that our little shop would be named Magnolia. I've always loved magnolia trees and their blooms—there's something so beautiful about a magnolia blossom. It demands attention, and you can't help but love those big, creamy petals and that fragrant smell. We'd handed out magnolia leaves at our wedding, and we'd had those two beautiful magnolia trees in the front yard of our first home together, so magnolias have always seemed like a part of us. Plus, they just seemed so entirely Southern. They reminded me of drinking sweet tea on the big wraparound porch of a nineteenth-century plantation home or something.

The name *Magnolia* just fit my business and the feeling I wanted to create. We loved it. But I really struggled with how to put the name on that sign. I figured I would have to hand-paint the thing since I didn't have a budget to have anything professionally made, and I just couldn't come up with anything that worked. I kept drawing things out, trying to write the word *Magnolia* in different ways, using the flower itself in a logo of sorts, and it just never felt right to me.

Then one day Chip showed up with the back of his pickup truck just loaded with old metal letters he'd found at a flea market—big, oddly shaped letters taken from various old signs. They were mismatched and rusty and dented—and I loved them. We tacked them up on the front of the shop, spelling out the name that would come to mean so much: *Magnolia.* The letters were uneven and looked a little handmade and ragged, but it seemed to work. I loved this sign because Chip designed it and made it with his own two hands. It came together in such an imperfectly perfect way, and I hoped people would get it.

To this day that sign is one of my proudest accomplishments. I'm no Joanna Gaines, but I certainly see things differently and love design in my own unique way. That first sign really reflected that for me. I would glow when I would hear a customer come in the shop and say, "I saw the sign and just had to stop in."

Finally, in October of 2005, the shop was ready to go. In a rush, I hand-painted a dinky little "Open" sign, but I ran out of space for the *n*, so it dropped down at the end. It was just bad. I didn't have an advertising budget. I hadn't done any marketing at all. We'd told plenty of people we knew, of course, and our parents had spread the word, but I was basically hoping that people would see my store when they were driving by and drop in. And yet I put out a sign on my opening day that looked like a four-year-old had drawn it. It was pathetic.

Inside, the shop was pretty much everything I wanted it to be. In addition to the home décor items, I had a section full of fresh flowers for sale. They smelled so good and looked perfect. When I was in New York, I had lived next to a little flower shop, and I'd loved watching people walk out with fresh flowers wrapped in kraft paper. I wanted to create that same feel in Waco, Texas that I had experienced in New York City.

So I had the flowers all ready to go. I had the candles burning. I had Frank Sinatra music playing. And at 9:55 a.m., just five minutes before the doors opened, I started to freak out.

She was hyperventilating. No joke. I thought I might have to take her to the emergency room or something, she was so nervous.

I just started panicking. "No one's going to come. Why is no one here?"

Chip and I had done the math. I needed to make at least two hundred dollars a day in order to pay the mortgage and insurance and electricity. That was two hundred dollars every day we were open just to stay afloat, without any profits. I'd been working so hard getting everything ready that I hadn't stopped to think about what might happen if the store didn't make that much money. I was close to a complete nervous breakdown, thinking, *What if this doesn't work?*

Then, just after ten o'clock, a Hummer pulled into the parking lot, followed by a Mercedes, followed by a Suburban and then a BMW. All these rich women showed up out of nowhere.

They were doctors' and lawyers' wives, stay-at-home moms and grandmothers who loved to shop and who did their best to make their homes feel nice. It turned out they'd all been watching my little shop come together during the renovations. They'd been eagerly anticipating my opening day for weeks, and it seemed that my idea of bringing a New York-style boutique experience to a home décor store wasn't far-fetched at all. There were a lot of people in town who were excited for it.

My first day open we made $2,800.

By the way, my dad decided to sell his Firestone shop shortly after this. I went over and helped him clean out the attic one day, and guess what I found up there? The wicker sleigh that I'd fixed up nice with the garland and Christmas lights and put up for sale in his lobby was still there, tucked in a corner. I just shook my head. He bought it himself to give me a little boost of confidence as I got ready to open my store.

What can I say? It worked. And so did the shop.

Sometimes when something is meant to be, it's meant to be. It had nothing to do with how I advertised, and it certainly didn't have anything to do with my being some kind of an amazing designer or having a reputation, because I wasn't any kind of a designer at all, and no one knew who I was. I just knew what I liked, and I trusted that other people might like it too. And I was where I was supposed to be. I'd listened to my own intuition and let God guide me toward the plans he'd had for me all along.

I mean, is there anyone who could possibly imagine that the way to get to your life's calling would be to marry a guy who showed up an hour and a half late to your first date and then to let that man talk you into opening your own small business in the first year of marriage? But guess what? It all seemed to be working out in that perfectly messy way life works when you trust in God and his plans for your life rather than focusing on your own.

At that point, I wasn't anywhere near used to the dynamics of it all. Chip's impulsive buying of properties, the way I'd hate them at first and then come to love them, only to have to move out again, the unexpected twists and turns and the hardships we'd have to overcome to get ourselves back on course—all of that was still new to me. And as we repeated them over the next few years, moving from flip house to flip house and starting over again and again, there would be a whole lot of tears.

But the fact that we established that crazy pattern of doing things in our own unique way so early on in our marriage was important. It prepared us for everything that would come later on. And Chip's decision to move us into that little white eight-hundred-square-foot house worked out exactly the way he said it would. It helped us to get ahead and start making some sustainable income.

One of the real pluses to that second house was it had a big side yard that we could subdivide, so we could build a whole second house to rent or to sell right next to the one we were living in. I bought that house, lot included, for $30,000, and we probably put $25,000 into it. So we were all-in for $55,000 on that little house, and it turned out beautiful—it really did. And we were able to build a brand-new house next door for about $130,000.

And of course this was all debt. We didn't own anything outright. And getting the money to do all this hadn't been easy. The banks hadn't wanted to mess around with these little houses at first. They were either small potatoes, or the banks felt I needed to build a reputation first. The few they actually agreed to caused us to go scrambling every month just to make the payments and pay our own bills.

When it came to remodeling, we never took out any walls or did any major construction at that point. Everything was just cosmetic. But we tried to do things creatively and nice. We updated the kitchen with new appliances. We used the existing cabinets and learned to repaint them. We put in new countertops and a new backsplash when we could. We restored the hardwood floors, and I mean lots of them. Chip literally became an expert in setting tile and wood floor restoration. We took out the bathtub and replaced it with a nice, wide shower with multiple showerheads and some body jets. Honestly, it felt luxurious, like the kind of shower you'd find in a really upscale house or a spa somewhere. Then came the paint, and we were done. And by that point, as I've mentioned, I would be in love with the place.

But it wasn't just the work we put in that made me love that tiny white house. It wasn't even the easy vacuuming, though that was a plus. What made that house special was the incredible memories we made there.

We threw Chip's thirtieth birthday party in that house's little backyard. I strung Christmas lights in the trees, and Chip built a firepit that was unbelievable. We didn't have much in the way of backyard furniture, so I put hay bales all around the perimeter for people to sit on. There was a little old weathered shed in the back, and I lit that up too.

It looked like something you'd see in a magazine. It was one of the best parties I've ever had in my life. It was funny because we were basically poor. We didn't know how we were going to pay our bills at the end of the month, and we were living in this tiny house, and I invited all of these college buddies to my party who'd gone and started making real money. They came in from Dallas and Austin and parked their Beemers and their Range Rovers up on the lawn of this $30,000 property we owned.

But we were proud of that house. We didn't think anything of it. We were excited to have all of our friends from college there to see what we'd been up to and to celebrate Chip's thirtieth birthday together.

I was thirty years old and still living by the seat of my pants. I probably should have had my life together a little bit more by then. But the thing was, my friends all had these stressed-out lives, and they came to our place and it felt like we were just living this laid-back, beautiful, no-stress life. We made being poor look fun. All these corporate friends of ours were thinking, *Well, maybe it wouldn't have been so bad to stay in Waco.*

It wasn't just my friends that made that party special, though. My grandma was still alive, and she came to that party too. She was just the sweetest lady in the world. She had single-handedly raised my dad and his brother. And though she had a very tough life, you would have never known it by her attitude. Between my mom and my grandma, I was definitely genetically built for positive optimism. That day with her is one of my fondest memories, because she and I hung out on one of those bales of hay for what felt like hours. It wasn't but a couple years after that she went to be with Jesus.

We made all kinds of big memories in that tiny house, and we were just getting started. The fact that we had some profits starting to roll in from my little shop on Bosque only added to the sense of security we were building.

It's hard to describe the feeling that comes with starting your own business. It really is so much work in the beginning that you lose yourself in it. You lose your sense of time, and you can't believe how quickly the days go by because there's no time to focus on much of anything else. But then you open the doors, and it's like you've given birth to this new thing that didn't exist before. Then when it starts to flourish, well, that's just icing on the cake. To get to see it live and breathe and to know that this thing you created out of thin air can put a smile on other people's faces is such a blessing.

There were some women who would come into that store and drop fifteen hundred dollars in a single visit. It was unbelievable. But I think one of the favorite customers I had in that first year of Magnolia was a woman who didn't ever buy a thing. She would just show up now and then and poke around, and she told me one time, "I just come here because I want to be in here. This place inspires me."

That was just about the greatest compliment I could ever imagine. She affirmed for me that I had accomplished exactly what I'd set out to do, and that made me even more passionate about creating an experience for my customers. I worked every day to come up with new touches that would make the experience memorable. I never got too comfortable with one particular look or design. I wanted to constantly challenge myself and make it better. If people were going to go out of their way to come into my store, I wanted to make sure it was worthwhile, whether they bought something or not.

Magnolia was my baby—no doubt about that. But it wasn't long before I found out it wasn't the only baby I was going to have.

SIX

WHITE PICKET FENCES

I've been asked from time to time how Chip and I manage to juggle all the things we did—and still do. I honestly don't have a good answer for that, other than to go back to the notion that we seem to energize one another when we're together. Although one explanation for where we find a little "extra" time in our days is the fact that since we got married we have never had a TV in our own house.

That is one question I always field on Twitter, "Hey man, why doesn't Joanna ever set up a TV in any of these homes?" I think they are implying I need to turn in my man card. But this is actually the answer to that question.

Before we got married, the two of us attended a few premarital counseling sessions with Chip's friend and one of his mentors, Byron Weathersbee, and his wife, Carla. Byron had played a significant part in Chip's life as a college student, and since then, Chip sought Byron's wisdom on lots of things. Chip and I felt that applying that same logic to our marriage—getting advice from these two trusted and seasoned marriage pros—couldn't be a bad thing. We wanted to start a habit of seeking outside opinions just to make sure we were thinking about everything a new couple ought to think about as we started our new life together.

One of the things Byron and Carla suggested was that we try to stay focused on each other and spend quality time doing things we loved together, especially when we were at home. That seemed like a no-brainer to us, but they explained that being in the same house and actually *interacting* with each other are two different things. Sometimes it's easy for couples to get lost in their own little worlds at home—to be so focused on other things that they aren't really together, even when they're in the same room.

To counter that tendency, Byron and Carla suggested we try to go the first few weeks of our marriage without a TV. The idea was to find other ways to occupy our time, especially in the evenings, with activities we could truly share. It seemed like reasonable advice, and so we tried it.

Well, six months later, neither one of us had the slightest urge to get a TV. We never even found time to miss it. All our various projects kept us busy during the day. And our evenings were pretty filled up with making dinner and finishing up the day's business, talking and dreaming together, and making plans for the next day or the next week. We couldn't imagine setting aside even an hour to sit and watch TV.

That's not to say we never slowed down. Reading a good book, flipping through magazines, learning new card games together, taking walks together—we found a million ways to enjoy some down time.

Now, to be fair, we've caught our share of TV at our friends' homes or at our parents'. Any time there was a big game or a fun show, we would find a way to catch it at a restaurant or make a date of it at a friend's house. So, we managed to catch up on some of our favorite shows through these outlets.

We've had more than thirteen years now without a TV, and I don't feel like we've missed a thing.

Just when we thought our lives couldn't get any busier—just as we'd settled into that little white house and my store was getting off the ground—I received the wonderful news that I was pregnant with our first child.

Just the thought of having a baby filled me with all sorts of new inspiration, not the least of which was imagining the room I wanted my baby to come home to. The tiny second bedroom in that eight-hundred-square-foot house needed a complete makeover to turn it into a nursery, and thinking about that actually spurred an idea that gave me a new perspective on decorating.

I had made the décor in our second home more cohesive than the ones in the yellow house. The colors were continuous, and the rooms all tied together rather than each space having its own theme. My store was so busy that I kept finding new furnishings and swapping them in and out between the store and our home, and I felt like I was starting to get a hang of this thing called decorating.

Once I found out I was having a boy, I zeroed in on earthy tones and a sort of outside-meets-inside theme in the room. Instead of the standard baby blue, I wanted something warm and comfortable that would reflect the rest of that luxurious little retreat we'd created. But I didn't have a lot of money to spend on that little nursery. Any money we made seemed to go right into another project or investment or just to keep up the payments on all the loans we'd taken out.

I realized we just couldn't afford any extra bells and whistles on that room, not even window treatments. I knew that window treatments can be expensive. But I decided to look at our tiny budget as a design challenge. I stood in the nearly finished nursery one day, just staring out the window, and I noticed the little white picket fence we'd put up in the front yard. An idea popped into my head immediately, "Hey, Chip, what would happen if you went and got some pieces of picket fence at the lumberyard and built an awning out of that wood for the inside of the nursery?"

I sketched it out for him, with the picket fence coming down at an angle from above the windows, kind of like an awning you'd see on the outside of a restaurant. Chip ran with it and figured out how to tack fencing to another board so he could hang it just so. We painted it, and it worked!

I stood back when we were done, looked at that room, and realized something big: having a tight budget doesn't have to mean watering down the design. If anything, it forced me to get *more* creative, and there was so much joy in that for me. I loved that awning Chip built way more than I ever would've loved a store-bought window treatment. It turned out perfect and taught me one of my fundamental design rules: don't be afraid to think outside of the box.

People liked those awnings so much that we actually started building them and selling them to our clients. For a season those things were hot!

Well, that was the other thing that happened. Beyond the house flipping and rental properties, we started picking up clients for remodels and redesigns.

As my baby bump grew behind the counter at the store, I found that more and more of those moms and grandmothers who came in to browse started bringing me pictures of rooms in their homes and asking for my advice. "I just don't like this room, and I don't know why," they would say. I would look at those pictures and suggest that maybe they could switch the furniture around or put up something interesting on a wall that had nothing but flat picture frames on it. I would recommend changing the wall color or adding a nice lamp in a nook or adding new throw pillows for a pop of color on the sofa.

It was a new challenge daily, but giving the advice sharpened my design skills, and I learned a few things about my own style in the process. It was an education for me. But more than that, it started to evolve into a second business.

Occasionally I'd point out that a room called for much more than new throw pillows, and the owner would ask, "Well, is that something you could do for me? I'd love to just hire you and Chip to come in and do the work!"

Between building the new house on our newly subdivided lot, continuing work on some small flip homes, and managing the rentals, Chip had more work than he could do himself, so he had put a crew of workmen together. "The Boys," as we called them, were a talented bunch of hardworking guys who were just as adaptable as Chip seemed to be when it came to making my crazy ideas become reality. I truly could say, "Hey, why don't we take that tree out of the front yard and hang it upside down in the master bedroom," and they would do it, no questions asked. (All right, maybe there'd be a little head scratching. But then they'd shrug their shoulders and get to work.) So between all of us, we picked up this occasional additional work doing interiors—painting, refinishing floors, basically redecorating for these new clients.

It wasn't easy to juggle it all, especially since I was running the store by myself that first year. But I loved every minute of it. There was no doubt in my mind that I was doing what I was meant to be doing.

I wonder sometimes if we know ourselves a lot better than we think we do when we're children. We get into our teen years and college years, and so many of us let others redefine who we are, or we get lost along the way and have no idea what we really want to do with our lives. But once we finally figure it out, it often seems easy to look back into our childhoods and find a few clues that say, "Hey, maybe you were headed in that direction all along."

For me, the entrepreneurial spirit was always there. During my young years in Wichita, Kansas, my mom worked at a little gift shop owned by one of her friends. After school my two sisters and I would go there while she worked, and I would always play store. I would sit there and pretend that I was working the cash register. I would have my sisters bring stuff up to the counter, and I would wrap it. I loved doing that. Even when we'd go home, I would set up my whole room like a store and then have fake customers come in. At one point I had a set of Lee Press-On Nails, and I would make my sisters come in like customers to a spa. I was always thinking about ways to make money, so I would basically make my sisters pay me for whatever they were buying, even if it was only a dime.

On the weekends I made a habit of setting up these makeshift little carnivals in our backyard and charging neighborhood kids a dollar to get in. I'd have lemonade and rides (primarily just the swing set) and games. To swing on the swing set would cost you another dime. But I always wanted it to be this fun experience for everyone, so I would work hard all week getting it set up.

My sisters basically provided free labor for me, in addition to having to pay to get in. I'm not sure why they went along with it, seeing that I was the middle child, but they did. Home was the place where I asserted myself, and I wasn't shy about it the way I was in other places. I felt safe at home and felt like I could be me.

I was also a creative kid, but not in terms of artistry or design or anything like that. I was just always pretending. I kept trying to invent wings so I could fly. I always wanted to come up with something that someone would buy. So I was always thinking.

I remember playing a lot by myself. My older sister and my younger sister, when they weren't being my minions, were usually out playing with the neighborhood kids, but I could usually be found in a corner playing make-believe. I pretended different things at different phases of my childhood. For a while I was always doing pretend commercials. So if I were eating breakfast, I would hold up the cereal box and say, "Kellogg's. We make this nutritious." I would read it like a newscaster and pretend that I was on a commercial. Sometimes I'd do the same thing with the bottle of shampoo in the shower. No matter where I was, I would act out these commercials as if I had a real audience.

That's another strange thing, considering what I'm doing now. Growing up, I sometimes felt like this audience of mine was always with me, watching me in my pretend store, watching me doing commercials. It was almost as if I was living in the *Truman Show,* that movie with Jim Carrey in which a character is filmed from the moment of birth and watched by millions as he goes through his daily life. Even if I was by myself, I would look around and think, *I know you are out there watching me.*

My parents remember hearing me talking to this unseen audience often when I was a little girl. They say I also swore I had a pet rabbit named Jo. But according to my parents, it was just make-believe. It was all the expression of a creative mind.

Anyway, looking back, I can see there were a whole bunch of things in my childhood that pointed toward what I'd do in my adult life. And once I started doing it "for real," I thrived. It seemed that the more opportunities I had to get creative and get entrepreneurial, the more fulfilled and energized I felt about life.

Outside of the store, Chip and I kept most of our endeavors in our typical wheelhouse. We sank our money and time into Third Street, where Chip continued to be the honorary "mayor" as he continued to expand his rental and home-building business.

A big part of Chip's dream for that street began in a deal he made before we were married. Chip and his father went in on a deal together to purchase eleven acres of land just a few blocks from where we would live as newlyweds. Chip was convinced that the Third Street area would go up in value. Baylor University was only about a mile away, just across La Salle Avenue. And eventually, Chip believed, Baylor would run out of room to house its growing student population.

Well, his intuition on that was right. A big out-of-town company came along and saw what Chip was doing with his few small rental houses in this mostly untouched area of Waco, and they made him an offer—a good offer—on those eleven acres. Their plan was to build hundreds of units of dorm-style apartment homes on Third Street to market to the Baylor community. They were basically going to create a whole new neighborhood on the land Chip and his dad had been sitting on.

Chip wasn't interested in selling all the land off. He had big dreams of owning rental homes up and down Third Street. So he structured a deal that sold off the back part of the acreage to that big company, while he kept the acreage along the road frontage to split into small lots where he could eventually build some individual rental houses himself.

Chip and his father made good money on that sale, and that allowed us to do some more investing, hire more help, and get started building some more little rental homes—basically sinking every penny that came into our long-term future. In our personal lives, we were still barely scraping by. But the business side of things was going well. In fact, we were seeing so much growth and progress on Third Street that there were times when we felt as if the whole neighborhood was ours.

Only it wasn't.

By this time we had three dogs—Shiner, Maggie, and Blue, all rescue mutts. It was too crowded in an eight-hundred-square-foot house to keep three dogs inside all the time, so we'd let those dogs out to roam around. They were a lot like me and pretty much thought they owned Third Street too. I had this four-wheeler that I'd ride up and down the street, just checking on everything, and those dogs would run right along with me.

They were some of the best dogs you've ever seen. They never bothered anyone, certainly never bit anyone or even came close. But we had this one neighbor across the street who hated those dogs, and every single time she saw them off leash—which was just about all the time—she called animal control.

The people from the pound would show up, haul the dogs downtown in their van, and write us a ticket either in Jo's name or my name. There were times when the officer would call the dogs right off of our front porch: "Come here, dogs!" They'd hop right in his van, and off they'd go, back for another stay in the pound.

These weren't like parking tickets either. They came with heavy fines, which I absolutely refused to pay out of some misguided form of principle. I never was much of a rule follower, and this "put your dog on a leash" rule was no exception. If the dogs had been hurting somebody, I'd have understood. But to take them from our own front yard?

Well, guess what? When you don't pay your fines, eventually the police come looking for you.

We owed something like twenty-five-hundred dollars in tickets, and we simply didn't have that kind of money lying around, even if we wanted to pay the fines. Especially since I was about to have a baby. Sure enough, two weeks early, I delivered a beautiful, healthy baby boy that we named Drake. We named him after the New York hotel where we'd stayed on our honeymoon.

So Drake was a week old, and I was sitting in this house, feeding him in the back room, when I heard a knock on the door. Chip answered it. It was the police.

"Is Joanna Gaines here? We have a warrant here for her arrest," the officer said.

It was the tickets. I knew it. And I panicked. I picked up my son and I hid in the closet. I literally didn't know what to do. I'd never even had a speeding ticket, and all of a sudden I'm thinking, *I'm about to go to prison, and my child won't be able to eat. What is this kid gonna do?*

I heard Chip say, "She's not here."

Thankfully, Drake didn't make a peep, and the officer believed him. He said, "Well, just let her know we're looking for her," and they left.

Jo's the most conservative girl in the world. She had never even been late for school. I mean, this girl was straitlaced. So now we realize there's a citywide warrant out for her arrest, and we're like, "Oh, crap." In her defense, Jo had wanted to pay those tickets off all along, and I was the one saying, "No way. I'm not paying these tickets." So we decided to try to make it right. We called the judge, and the court clerk told us, "Okay, you have an appointment at three in the afternoon to discuss the tickets. See you then." We wanted to ask the judge if he could remove a few of them for us. The fines for our dogs "running at large" on our front porch just seemed a bit excessive.

We arrived at the courthouse, and Chip was carrying Drake in his car seat. I couldn't carry it because I was still recovering from Drake's delivery. We got inside and spoke to a clerk. They looked at the circumstances and decided to switch all the tickets into Chip's name.

Those dogs were basically mine, and it didn't make sense to have the tickets in her name. But as soon as they did that, this police officer walked over and said, "Hey, do you mind emptying out all of your pockets?"

I got up and cooperated. "Absolutely. Yep," I said. I figured it was just procedure before we went in to see the judge.

Then he said, "Yeah, you mind taking off your belt?"

I thought, *That's a little weird.*

Then he said, "Do you mind turning around and putting your hands behind your back?"

They weren't going to let us talk to the judge at all. The whole thing was just a sting to get us to come down there and be arrested. They arrested Chip on the spot. And I'm sitting there saying, "I can't carry this baby in his car seat. What am I supposed to do?"

I started bawling. "You can't take him!" I cried. But they did. They took him right outside and put him in the back of a police car.

Now I feel like the biggest loser in the world. I'm in the back of a police car as my crying wife comes out holding our week-old baby.

I'm walking out, limping, and waving to him as they drive away.

And I can't even wave because my hands are cuffed behind my back. So here I am awkwardly trying to make a waving motion with my shoulder and squinching my face just to try to make Jo feel better.

It was just the most comical thing, honestly. A total joke. To take a man to jail because his dogs liked to walk around a neighborhood, half of which he owns? But it sure wasn't funny at the time. I was flooded with hormones and just could not stop crying. They told me they were taking my husband to the county jail.

Luckily we had a buddy who was an attorney, so I called him. I was clueless. "I've never dated a guy that's been in trouble, and now I've got a husband that's in jail. What do I do? What's the first step here?" I asked. He made some calls, and he told me that I could get Chip out with a bail bond for eight hundred dollars.

It couldn't be done with a personal check, and we didn't have eight hundred dollars in the bank anyway. I needed eight hundred dollars in cash to go buy a money order at the gas station near the facility in order to get Chip out of jail, and I didn't have the money to do it. My parents or his parents would have given us that money in a heartbeat, I'm sure, but I was too embarrassed. I didn't want our parents to know we didn't have eight hundred dollars between us, and I certainly didn't want them knowing Chip was in the slammer.

Thankfully, I had my shop. I went and I emptied out both the cash register and the safe in the back. I didn't know how I'd make change the next day, and I had no idea how we'd make up for that loss when it came time to pay the bills. But I had no choice. It was the only money I had.

Off I went to the gas station. Then I went to the jail with my week-old son strapped to my chest in his BabyBjörn and waited. And waited.

Chip had been in there for a few very long hours. I had all kinds of awful thoughts about what might have happened to him in there. What if he'd been roughed up? Strip-searched? Who knows what awful things could have happened in a place like that? I saw scary-looking characters come and go as I sat in that cold, concrete lobby, trying to make myself invisible.

Finally, out came Chip.

"Hi, baby. Thanks for bailing me out," he said.

He sounded almost chipper.

"Are you okay?"

"Yeah, yeah! You'll never guess who I saw in there. Alfonzo! Remember the lawn guy who used to work for me? We had a good time catching up."

Only Chip could go to prison and come out talking about all the friends he'd run into there.

I came out and I was like, "Whoa! That was awesome. Jo, I met this guy. He did this thing. You know this old guy that I used to tell you about—he and I used to work together? He's doing great. Well, he's in jail, but things are really good otherwise."

Two of the policemen were also buddies of mine. These guys were literally standing on the other side of these bars going, "Why are you here? What's the deal?" We had this endearing conversation right there, while I was in a jail cell.

I used to live out in the boonies when I was in college, and I had mowed this one guy's grass. So I told him what I was in for. "Long story short, I got these dogs running around." And he was like, "Oh, dude, you'll be fine. I'm sure they'll get you right out of here."

It was just another day in my new life with Chip Gaines. But that was the moment I realized that we were right on the edge of a real financial struggle, and I didn't like that feeling.

I have a naturally conservative nature, and Chip and I were supposed to balance each other out, not concede to each other's strengths and weaknesses. My strength is saving and being tight with the money, but I had not exercised that strength recently. I had let my head get in the clouds and forgotten that this was important.

Not having the money to pay for those tickets in the first place should have been a wake-up call. Having to scrape the bottom of our barrel for bail money was certainly cause for alarm. I promised myself I would start putting money aside for future emergencies.

I don't think it's irrational or too conservative of me to think, *I never want to carry my baby into the county jail ever again.*

Is it?

SEVEN

ONE DOOR CLOSES

The very next week, I got back to work. I needed to get back in the shop and start making some sales to recoup the money we'd pulled out for bail and then to pay off the rest of those tickets. I didn't have a babysitter or the money to pay one. So I started working every day with a two-week-old baby.

We set up a little nursery area in the back office with a Pack 'n Play portable crib, and I worked the register with Drake in his BabyBjörn. I would run to the back office to feed him, and then, of course, a customer would walk in. So I'd have to wrap up the feeding session, which would make him cry.

I knew I needed to get some help at the shop. I couldn't do all of this by myself anymore.

Thank God for Jessica! She was a good friend from college, one of the two sets of twins in our wedding. And best of all, she was available. I hired her on to assist behind the register, and that gave me a little bit of freedom. Jessica had a way about her that made every customer feel warm and welcome. I was thankful for her diligence and friendship during that time when I was both a new mom and a new business owner.

Just as Drake turned six weeks old, I decided I wanted to lose some baby weight. Chip and I were both still getting used to the idea that we had a baby of our own now, but I felt it was okay to leave him with Chip for a half hour or so in the mornings so I could take a short run up and down Third Street. I left Drake in the little swing he loved, kissed Chip good-bye, and off I went.

Chip was so sweet and supportive. When I got back he was standing in the doorway saying, "Way to go, baby!" He handed me a banana and asked if I'd had any cramps or anything. I hadn't. I actually felt great.

I walked in and discovered Chip had prepared an elaborate breakfast for me, as if I'd run a marathon or something. I hadn't done more than a half-mile walk-run, but he wanted to celebrate the idea that I was trying to get myself back together physically. He'd actually driven to the store and back and bought fresh fruit and real maple syrup and orange juice for me.

I sat down to eat, and I looked over at Drake. He was sound asleep in his swing, still wearing nothing but his diaper. "Chip, did you take Drake to the grocery store without any clothes on?"

Chip gave me a real funny look. He said, "What?"

I gave him a funny look back.

"Oh my gosh," he said. "I totally forgot Drake was here. He was so quiet."

"Chip!" I yelled, totally freaked out.

I was a first-time mom. Can you imagine?

Anyone who's met Chip knows he can get a little sidetracked, but this was our child!

He was in that dang swing that just made him perfectly silent. I felt terrible. It had only been for a few minutes. The store was just down the street. But I literally got on my knees to beg for Jo's forgiveness.

Several days later I decided to go on a good long jog, trusting that Chip would not leave Drake again. As I was on my way back I saw Chip coming down the road in his truck with the trailer on it. He rolled up to me with his window down and said, "Baby, you're doing so good. I'm heading to work now. I've got to go."

I looked in the back, thinking, *Of course, he's got Drake.* But I didn't see a car seat.

"Chip, where's Drake?" she said, and I was like, "Oh, shoot!" She took off without a word and ran like lightning all the way back to the house as I turned the truck around. She got there faster on foot than I did in my truck.

I sure hope no one from Child Protective Services reads this book. They can't come after me retroactively, can they?

Chip promised it would never happen again. So the third time I attempted to take a run, I went running down Third Street and made it all the way home. I walked in, and Chip and Drake were gone. I thought, *Oh, good. Finally he remembered to take the baby.* But then I noticed his car was still parked out front. I looked around and couldn't find them anywhere.

Moments later, Chip pulled up on his four-wheeler—with Drake bungee-strapped to the handlebars in his car seat. "Chip!" I screamed, "What in the heck are you doing?"

"Oh, he was crying, and I'd always heard my mom say she would drive me around the neighborhood when I was a baby, and it made me feel better," Chip said. "He loved it. He fell right to sleep."

"He didn't love it, Chip. He probably fell asleep because the wind in his face made it impossible to breathe."

I didn't go for another run for the whole first year of Drake's life, and I took him to the shop with me every single day. Some people might see that as a burden, but I have to admit I loved it. Having him in that BabyBjörn was the best feeling in the world.

Drake was a shop baby. He would come home every night smelling like candles.

We had friends who owned a barbecue joint, and their baby always came home smelling like a rack of ribs. I liked Drake's smell a whole lot better.

A lot of my clientele seemed to have kids who were older, and I swear every single one of those moms would smile and coo over Drake, saying, "Joanna, this goes by so fast. You need to embrace these moments. My kids are getting ready to go off to college, and it feels like just yesterday they were little like this." And as much as they loved shopping at my store, some of my best customers kept saying, "You should think about taking some time off—maybe close up shop for a while. This is a moment in time you'll never get back. Don't work too much. Make sure you're all-in with your baby."

I didn't listen at first. What new mom does? It seems as if every day lasts forever when you're up all night with feedings and changing smelly diapers. But the more I heard those words, the more they started to sink in.

Toward the end of 2005, Chip came across an opportunity to buy a nice lot just up the road from where we lived. He knew how cramped we were in that little white house, and even though he felt as though any money we made should be reinvested in the business and rolled into the next project, he asked me one day if maybe we should invest in building a house of our own.

"Yes!" I said. I *loved* that idea.

Chip was pretty certain he could get the financing together for the house if we bought the land, but the parcel of land was $5,000, and he wasn't sure how we were going to get it before somebody else snatched it up.

That's when I surprised him. Ever since the jail incident, I had been saving a little money here and there from my sales at the shop. I just set it away where neither of us would touch it until there was something important to use it on, just for us.

78

The amount of money I had saved was exactly $5,000—just what we needed to buy that land. So we went for it, and together we designed a comfortable, sixteen-hundred-square-foot home from the ground up. I loved designing this home from the beginning stages.

I learned that, unlike the older homes we had renovated, a new home doesn't come with oak floors, thick trim, and built-in character. And I learned pretty quickly that adding character was expensive. If I wanted our place to be special and unique, I had to get creative. On the exterior, for instance, we wanted rock, but could only afford enough for the front of the house. So we added larger trees in the landscape to hide the side elevation and draw attention to the front door.

Speaking of that front door, Chip had to get creative himself. Buying things for clients was one thing, but buying stuff for our house was a different story. We had this charming arched door, crafted out of solid mesquite wood, that Chip had bought from a guy whose shop was going out of business. The best thing about this door was it had a peep door at the top that you could open so you could see who was on the other side. It felt very Hansel and Gretel. This amazing door brought the perfect balance to the heavy rock exterior—made it feel like a quaint rustic cottage.

On the inside, we couldn't afford the oak wood floors I loved, so we opted for stained concrete. I didn't want the room to look too cold, so we ended up scoring the concrete in a large diagonal pattern that made the floors look like a million bucks. We had some exterior rock left over, so I decided to mount the remaining pieces as a chair rail under our bar top, which Chip had constructed from reclaimed wood. Eventually it all came together, and we thought it was beautiful. It was so rewarding to stay on budget but have a house that was unique in its own special way.

In 2006 we moved in, and the layout worked so well that we decided our house would make the perfect model for a new set of student rental homes. We figured we could fit eight of those houses along the frontage parcels Chip had retained after selling part of the eleven acres to that big, out-of-town development company. But building those houses would mean getting a bigger line of credit and expanding Chip's ragtag home-building and house-flipping business into more of a bona fide company.

This house-building business quickly became more than Chip's company. It became *our* company, a true fusion of what he was doing and what I was doing. We decided to call it Magnolia Homes.

It was right around that time when I found out I was pregnant with our second child. This time it was going to be a girl. We decided to name her Ella Rose.

Sales at my shop were better in my second year than they'd been in the first. I was building a reputation and a steady client base, and I felt like I was starting to actually know what I was talking about in terms of design.

I loved that shop. I loved being there every day. Yet once I was pregnant with Ella, I heard a voice. Remember the voice on our first date, the one that told me Chip was the man I would marry? This was the same voice. But this time it was saying, *Jo, it's time to stay home with your babies.*

I didn't really want to hear that. In fact, I argued with the voice, just as I had argued about what it said about Chip. "No, I can't," I said. "I'm finally getting this! It's working!"

And it *was* working, better than I ever expected. That shop meant something to a lot of people, and I'm not just talking about me and my clientele.

It seemed that wherever we went and whatever we did, Chip would always find some kids to mentor along the way. One late night we were at the shop unboxing some candles that had just come in, and Chip noticed two young boys walking through our parking lot. They were all of ten years old.

"Hey, guys," he said. "It's late! What are you guys doing out here on the streets at this time of night?"

They said they lived in the neighborhood behind the shop, and they always walked around at night. So Chip said, "Hey, you want to make a little bit of money?"

Of course the boys said yes. He invited them to come help us with inventory and gave them work sweeping and doing some other chores for a few bucks an hour. We always seemed to find ourselves at the shop doing something late at night, so those boys started dropping by regularly. "Hey, Chip and JoJo!" they'd say. "Got any work for us?"

Being able to mentor those kids just added to the value of being at the shop. I loved that. It was such a good feeling to see those kids fired up about doing some work rather than wandering around after dark, where trouble was sure to find them.

What I'm trying to say is that I truly loved *everything* about that shop. But the voice just kept on telling me, *Jo, it's time.*

I wrestled with it for weeks until finally I felt it in my heart. I thought about the words of all of those women who were in my shop every day, telling me to cherish this time with my child. Soon I would have two children whose time deserved cherishing.

As much as I didn't want it to be true, I could no longer deny that the voice was right.

I'm the type of person who can wrestle with something for a long time, but when I finally make up my mind, I'm all-in. This was one of those times. I was lying in bed with Chip one night, and I spoke it out loud. I didn't pose it as a question. It wasn't something I needed advice on. I was resolved: "Chip, we're shutting the shop down."

Chip was curious as to why I had come to this decision, of course. And I told him confidently, "God told me to do it."

How could he argue with that?

In March of 2006 we sold off everything—the inventory, the displays, even the cash register. And it was *hard*. That shop was my dream, a dream that had landed on my yellow steno pad after I came back from my eye-opening internship in New York City. It was the first dream of mine that I'd seen come to fruition, and in many ways it was like our first baby.

Chip and I had remodeled that old shop with our bare hands. We'd laughed about how many nails had been driven into the old floorboards—there were thousands of them!—and thought about the guy who had put in so much time and effort all those years ago just to make sure those floors were as solid as could be. We were proud of everything we'd done to accentuate the work of those who came before us and to turn that quirky little building into a shop that exceeded the dreams I'd drawn out on paper a few years earlier.

But the shop was more to me than an accomplishment or even the fulfillment of a dream. It was something Chip and I had dreamed and accomplished *together*. From scratch. It wasn't his business that I added to, or my business that he added to. It was *ours*. At some point every day, no matter what he had going on out at the various job sites, Chip had been there with me, sitting in that little back office at the desk right next to the Pack 'n Play, doing his thing while I did mine.

I will remember 'til the day I die the moment I stood on the front steps and locked that shop door for the last time as tears rolled down my face.

Even as I stood on those steps, trying to say good-bye, I kept asking God, "Are you sure this is the right move? If it is, why does it seem so painful and hard?"

That's when I heard that gentle whisper, *Joanna, if you trust me with your dreams, I'll take them further than you could have ever imagined.*

It is no easy thing to trust in God, to walk away from a career, to give it all up not knowing if you can ever get it back or even come close. But I did it. I heeded his voice, and somehow I found peace about it.

We put the shop on the market and hoped to find a buyer for that property as soon as possible. Obviously we wanted to respect it, the way Maebelle had respected it when she sold it to us. We still loved Maebelle, who had become like a grandmother to us. We used to visit her in the nursing home where she lived now and be her guests when they had pancake suppers.

But we just couldn't afford to hold on to the building out of principle, the way she had.

We both would have loved for someone to have saved that old building we'd worked so hard to fix up, but there just wasn't another Chip and Joanna out there who were looking for a property like that one. We couldn't keep paying a mortgage on a shop that wasn't open. So we told ourselves, "It is what it is. We need to move on. We'll see what happens." If someone came along and made us a decent offer, we would just have to cross that bridge when we came to it.

We considered offers from some other developers and business owners and kept trying to make a deal. But for some reason, those deals kept falling through.

What's interesting to me is that just as Jo closed up the shop, Magnolia Homes was starting to rock and roll. At the very same moment we were trying to sell that building, we were also looking for some office space for the company. We needed a place where we could hire a secretary to do the books. But we also needed a spot with some outdoor space where we could store supplies and materials, and possibly have a staging area for "the Boys" to gather what they needed before heading to a particular job site for a day.

I was out driving around with a buddy of mine who'd been helping me look for a good location, and he'd actually found a couple of spots around town, but we had never found a spot that jumped out at me.

We happened to turn down Bosque as we were driving, and he asked me, "What's the deal with the shop? Have you sold it yet?"

I told him we'd hit a few snags and hadn't been able to close a deal. And right as we were driving past it, he said, "Well, have you ever thought about using that for your office?"

It was like a giant lightbulb went on over my head. I swung the truck back around and pulled into the parking lot. I looked at that building with a whole new set of eyes. It had the parking lot in the front, but there was also an area in the back that was plenty big enough for a storage unit that could hold the lumber and materials we kept on hand or anything else we might need to store. It had an office in the back that was ready to go. And why couldn't we turn the front part, where the retail shop had been, into more office space too? The mortgage we were paying on that little building was less than the rent I'd be paying by a pretty good margin.

"Dude, you're a genius!" I said.

The very next day we jumped in and started renovating that store into the Magnolia Homes headquarters, adding the office and storage space that would make it home for our construction company.

Funny that we needed an outsider to bring that to our attention. We had always seen the building as our shop. But now it was "our" headquarters, and we were getting to hold on to that precious building. We could even keep our Magnolia sign.

It felt right. The whole thing felt right. Being at home as a full-time mom meant giving up the shop, but it didn't mean giving up on everything else.

Chip and I started working more closely together than ever. My design ideas were the backbone of Magnolia Homes, and I'd wind up coming in and out of that construction office as often as Chip had been in and out of the back office when it was my store. In the coming months, I'd actually figure out a way to stay in touch with all of my clientele and my wholesalers and to continue Magnolia as a home-furnishings brand without having a physical shop too.

I felt good about having made the decision to walk away and lock that door. It's funny, though, looking back on it now, because one very simple concept in life never occurred to me as I was walking away:

Even locked doors can be unlocked in time.

I simply never could have imagined just how much God had in store for us, and I certainly couldn't have dreamed just how many keys to other doors God had already placed in our hands.

EIGHT

DOWN TO OUR ROOTS

F or the next four years, Chip and I were dedicated to one thing: raising our beautiful babies.

In addition to Drake and Ella Rose, who was born in October of 2006, our family would come to include two more children, Duke and Emmie, who were born in 2008 and 2010, respectively. But when talking about our "babies," we also mean our business. The reach of Magnolia Homes quickly expanded beyond our little neighborhood on Third Street and into other areas all over Waco.

We had the opportunity to do all sorts of remodeling and renovation projects in a wide variety of homes, including some beautiful old homes in a historic part of town called Castle Heights. We did work there for some of the people who had frequented my now-closed shop—the wives of doctors and lawyers. And then, when they saw what we were capable of doing, those folks spread the word to neighbors and friends who had money to invest in more extensive remodeling projects.

This wasn't just changing throw pillows and paint colors. We put Chip's growing expertise to work and added the capability and muscle the Boys brought to the table to start tearing down walls, installing French doors, and creating new entryways—all catered to our clients' tastes through the filter of my own evolving design aesthetic.

Driving through the Castle Heights neighborhood, I was immediately drawn to it. I think almost anyone would be. It was full of beautiful, stately old homes with well-kept lawns, mostly tucked back off the main roads where there wasn't much traffic, so kids could play and ride bikes in the streets. And it wasn't a snobby sort of place either. Neighbors seemed to know each other, and their kids played together regularly. It seemed out of reach for us, and yet once we started working in those homes, I quickly started to dream about living in that neighborhood.

"*Someday*," I said to Chip.

And, well, you already know how my "somedays" worked out when I spoke them out loud to Chip. But I'll share a little more about that in a bit.

Looking back on those years, the thing that strikes me is that it all seemed to happen so fast. Maybe it was just a lack of sleep from having four kids in quick succession, but those years just seem to blur together for me.

I suppose a lot of young couples feel that way once kids come into the picture. Time does fly, just as those other moms had told me.

Every time I turned around, it seemed as though Drake had suddenly grown another inch or Ella Rose had started walking, or Duke and Emmie were sleeping through the night. These huge milestones came one on top of the other, and I felt truly blessed to be able to work from home so I never missed one—not to mention getting to work alongside my husband as we grew our business together.

The magic that Chip and I had discovered early on—that we seem to grow stronger the more time we spend together—never seemed to wear off. We were well past the honeymoon stage in our marriage, and yet we seemed to fall even more in love with each other now that we had children. We both fell more in love with our work, too, with every new project we tackled as a team.

Don't get me wrong. Juggling that sort of entrepreneurial career with four little kids was not easy. It seemed that no matter how hard we worked, no matter how many extra jobs we picked up, we were still barely scraping by and living with huge amounts of debt. Chip never stopped pulling crazy stunts, and each time I'd get just as angry over them as I'd gotten when he left Drake home alone those two times in his first few months.

But we always worked things out. Always. If we hadn't had each other to lean on, I don't know how we would have gotten through it all.

With two, then three, then four kids in the house, there wasn't very much time to think about the hows and whys of what made our relationship or our business tick. It seemed like everything just kept moving along. Thank goodness we had built our life on a strong foundation.

I think it was more than just the foundation of our own relationship, though. Part of what made Chip and I work so well together was clearly buried down deep in our roots. It came from our families and our upbringings and the challenges we'd already tackled within ourselves before we even met.

I've already mentioned that my early years were spent in Wichita, Kansas. That's where I was born in 1978, the middle of three girls. Teresa, the oldest, and Mary Kay (Mikey), the youngest, are still my closest friends today. But the roots I'm talking about really go back somewhere in the DNA of my parents, two completely unique people who met and fell in love back in 1969.

My dad was drafted to serve in Vietnam that year, when nearly all of the men who were drafted were sent straight to combat. But not my dad. He was held back in his class because of a case of shingles and ended up being sent to Seoul, Korea, six months later than originally planned.

During Dad's first few months overseas, while at a party with his friends, he met my mom for the first time. Though she was taking English classes at the time, she wasn't able to speak much just yet. But she was fascinated by the American culture, which she'd been exposed to from watching American movies. It seemed to her that women weren't treated with the kind of respect in Korea that they were in America. She hoped that by learning the language she'd learn more about the culture as a whole.

Interestingly enough, the way my mother tells it, she spotted my dad sitting off by himself in a corner at that party and said to a friend of hers, "That's the man I'm going to marry." Her friends thought she was crazy, but she says she just knew.

She wound up hanging around my dad and his friends a lot after that night. As it turned out, one of his good friends really liked her, but she always knew my dad was the one. After a few months they finally started dating—just before it was time for Dad to fly home.

Once he was back in America, the two of them began writing letters back and forth to each other. Whenever a new letter arrived, my dad would take it to a translator to have her words read to him, and she would do the same whenever his letters arrived in Seoul.

Everything was going well until my dad sent her an airline ticket and a letter that said, "Will you marry me? Come to America." Then my mother got a case of cold feet. It was what she'd always dreamed about, but it was a life-changing decision for her to make—and she had to make it fast.

Of course, ultimately she came and joined him in America, and he went to the Los Angeles airport to pick her up. They were married by a justice of the peace in Las Vegas in 1972 and then went to live in Wichita, Kansas, my dad's hometown. My dad had been raised Catholic and my mom had been raised Buddhist Korean, so neither set of parents approved of the marriage in the beginning.

From what they've told me, they actually had a rocky marriage for several years. My dad experimented with drugs, as many did back in the seventies, and this behavior was an issue between them. Communicating with one another over a cultural and language divide was surely a challenge as well. There were times, they say, when they didn't think they would make it because all they did was fight.

It wasn't until my father lost his grandmother, shortly before I was born, that he had an awakening of sorts. He was at her house after she'd passed away and was having a pretty bad trip. He envisioned himself in a casket, with his family surrounding him, and it hit him just how wrongly he was living his life. He knew he didn't want to end up in that casket the way he envisioned, leaving my mom alone to fend for herself. So he ran out of his grandmother's house and pleaded to God, "If you let me live, I promise I will turn my life around."

Through this promise, my parents discovered a faith in God from which there was no turning back. The two of them began memorizing Scripture together each day. This practice helped them discover new wisdom, and their marriage found itself on solid footing for the first time, and continued from that point forward.

My dad's father, my grandfather, had worked three jobs to support his big family of kids. By watching him, my dad had picked up a strong work ethic that kicked fully into gear right around the time I was born. That's when he went to work for Firestone, and every promotion after that meant moving our whole family to a new town.

By the time we got to Waco, Dad owned his own Firestone dealership, which was a dream come true for him. By that point my family had lived in seven or eight different houses, from Wichita to Corpus Christi, Texas, to Round Rock, just outside of Austin, Texas. Each one of those moves was a family decision. He sat us all down and discussed it every time, and each time we kind of knew it was coming. We were always sad to leave those places that had become home for us, but we were also always happy for dad and his pursuit of bigger and better opportunities.

Moving was never easy for me, though. This was due in part to my own insecurities, which trace back to my experiences in first or second grade back in Rose Hill, Kansas, when kids started noticing that I didn't look exactly like they did.

As a small child I had never noticed there was anything different about me. I thought I looked like everybody else. And really, most people don't look at me and automatically think I'm half-Korean. But in those first couple of years in elementary school, kids started picking on me because of it.

The worst of it came in the lunchroom. I would get served the same broccoli-and-cheese rice that everyone else in the lunch line was served. But a group of boys—especially this one redheaded boy—would start saying things like "Oh, look at the little Asian girl eating rice." Going to the lunchroom caused me so much anxiety that I asked my mom to start packing me a cold lunch instead. The kids who ate cold lunch gathered in a separate room, where it wound up just being me and a handful of other girls.

I thought I was in the clear then—until my grandmother came to live with us for a while and started attending school events. She looked like a traditional grandmother from South Korea. It was her first time in the United States, she wore no makeup, and all the children seemed to notice how different she looked from the average Kansas grandma. This seemed to give that group of boys more reason to make fun of me.

As a child I didn't know how to process all this. I just felt the pain of being different, and I felt I had to be something else in order to be accepted.

Luckily, kids grow out of that unfiltered phase, and the torment soon just sort of went away. The rest of my elementary school and middle school years were pretty normal. They were fun. Getting picked on for being different wasn't an issue I consciously carried with me as I grew. It wasn't something I worried about. I always made friends, and for years that old fear of walking into the cafeteria stayed buried somewhere deep in my subconscious.

Moving every few years left me feeling like I could never get comfortable, though. Just when I started to settle in somewhere and find my footing, I'd wake up, and it would be time to move again. I learned to just accept it. I trained myself to get used to it. And I suppose that set me up for my life with Chip in a big way. We may not have been making cross-country moves in our marriage, but moving from house to house is still a big change, and we would make a lot of those transitions.

I think the toughest move of all for me as a kid was between Corpus Christi and Round Rock. It happened during my sophomore year of high school. I'd gone to private school most of my life, so I was used to having maybe thirty people in my class. When I moved to Round Rock High School, there were nearly *six hundred* kids in my class. This came as a complete culture shock to me. We also moved in the middle of the year, and that made it even tougher, especially on the first day.

I had always made friends easily on my first day of school. When you're the new girl at a private school, everyone's excited to see a new face. But being the new girl at a large public school in Texas was different. I swear no one even noticed me. I wondered if they even noticed that I was new. For all they knew, I could have been there for years and just blended in.

I walked into the lunchroom on that first day at Round Rock High, and every bad feeling I had felt as a second grader came flooding back. I was literally crippled by it. In my mind I saw myself in a spotlight, a little girl walking into that crowd of people who would surely look at me as different. I was sure they were going to make fun of me.

In reality, I don't think anyone even noticed me, but I still felt awful. I walked through that cafeteria without making eye contact with anybody, went straight into the bathroom, and hid in a stall. I stayed in there for thirty minutes, right up until I heard the bell ring.

I wound up doing that every day for the rest of the semester, from January through May. I spent lunchtime either hiding in the bathroom or ducking into a quiet corner of the library.

I'm not sure why I was so terrified. Maybe it was just teenage hormones, but I never even gave those kids a chance to ask me to sit with them. I felt their rejection and acted on it before I even gave them a chance.

At some point my mom realized I wasn't eating lunch. She got mad at me at first. Then she said, "I'm going to pick you up. You have to eat." Sophomores weren't allowed to leave campus at lunchtime, so I had to sneak off campus to jump into my mom's getaway car. Once or twice a week we'd plan it so she'd be there at 11:15 on the dot. I would bolt out and jump over the rope at the edge of the lawn. My mom would have the car door open, waiting for me, and we'd take off. She'd take me to Wendy's and then secretly drop me back at school before the start of the next period. And each time she'd say, "Jo, listen, we can't keep doing this. You've got to make friends."

Mom wasn't enabling my fearful behavior. It was simply her motherly instinct; she wanted her teenage daughter to eat. As a mother now myself, I can't blame her. And now, looking back, those lunches stand out as some of my favorite times with my mother. We were kind of like lunchtime bandits, stealing away for twenty minutes together to laugh and talk and grab a burger together.

Over the course of the summer, I did make a few friends, and by the start of the next school year it all sort of worked itself out. It took me a good six months of awkwardness to finally find a friend group through gymnastics—and then we up and moved again in the middle of my junior year.

I arrived at my small private school in Waco (in a class of twenty-eight people) on the same day a group of Chinese exchange students were visiting the school. Everyone mistakenly thought I was one of them—a Chinese girl who just happened to dress American and didn't have an accent. Everyone was kind of intrigued by that. It served as an icebreaker that gained me some friendships from the get-go.

Right after we moved to Waco was when I started working with my dad at the Firestone dealership and started to get involved both at school and at church. It wasn't until my senior year, though, that I first started to think consciously about what it meant to be half-Korean.

I remember thinking, *I'm either white, Korean, or both, but I've got to own this. It's* me. I started to see how beautiful my mom's culture was and how beautiful she was, and there were times when I wanted people to know she was different and she was unique. I didn't want to be embarrassed about that.

To my surprise, in the fall of my senior year I was actually elected as our high school's homecoming queen. I remember walking out on the football field to be crowned, thinking about how radically different this feeling was from the rejection I'd felt just two years prior, hiding in bathroom stalls at lunchtime. I was thankful my high school career had ended on a good note. I felt there was redemption in my heart from an old wound that had never truly healed.

A few years later I graduated from Baylor University as a communications major, traveled to New York, and finally got rid of the second-grade chip on my shoulder. After all those years of failing to understand or embrace what an honor it was to be a part of my mother's amazing culture, I finally believed it was actually a beautiful thing to be unique and to be different.

And this, of course, was right around the time when Mr. Different-and-Unique himself, Chip Gaines, walked into my life.

NINE

CHIPPING IN

As I mentioned earlier, my mom and dad grew up in Archer City, Texas, a town of maybe two thousand people. When compared to Archer City, Waco would have been like the big city where you would come see a movie on the weekend or something.

My parents aren't ashamed to tell anybody that their whole group of friends in that town were all poor growing up, but my dad was the poorest kid of the bunch. He lived in what would be the equivalent of the projects in that town, and the government paid a portion of the rent for the apartment where he grew up.

His mom, my grandma, was a single mom raising two kids back in the day. In a town where everybody was broke, they were known as the poor family. So to my dad, my mom seemed like a rich girl just because her dad was a rancher and they had a house and some cows.

The two of them started dating in the eighth grade, and their small-town romance never let up. In those days, in that town, just a few folks had gone to college; no one's mom had gone to college. Nobody even thought about college, and even if they had wanted to go, no one could have afforded it. College wasn't really an option.

My dad would probably have graduated high school and become a mechanic or something like that. But then he started playing football, and he was good at it. He received a football scholarship to the University of New Mexico, and the whole world opened up to him.

He went off to Albuquerque, and to his small-town mind it was as big of a change as moving to Las Vegas or New York might be to somebody else. I mean, to him it was just the coolest place in the world. He got himself out of Texas for the first time ever and started learning about who he really was. The school was in the Western Athletic Conference (WAC), which played Hawaii, so he got to go to Hawaii. Twice. Before that, he had never even been on a plane!

My mom stayed in Texas and wound up going to a nearby college called Midwestern State. She and Dad carried on a long-distance relationship for two years. Then she transferred to UNM so they could be together—the football star and the cheerleader, the polar opposite of Jo's parents in many ways.

When my dad stayed on as a fifth-year senior, they got married, and my older sister, Shannon, came along shortly thereafter.

My dad was so excited and motivated by sports and athletics that, after he graduated, he opened a sporting goods store there in Albuquerque, the city where I was born in 1974. My parents tell me that even way back then I had a way of making friends with just about everybody, and I always wanted to do things for others. I was always asking my mom for money to give the homeless people we passed on the streets. And whenever some kid would come knocking on the door, trying to sell something, I'd say yes before he even started his pitch—then go running into the back of the house to get the money.

"Why do you need five dollars, Chip?" my parents would ask.

"Because I already bought this thing. This kid needs the money. Please!"

For some reason, even as a kid, I didn't qualify people like most folks do. I treated everybody the same. From a young age I understood the true meaning of the golden rule. I literally treated others as I wanted to be treated.

It probably comes as a surprise to no one that I had a certain wild streak as a kid. I had this great friend named Devon who lived directly across the street from me in our cookie-cutter suburban neighborhood. Our driveways sloped down toward the street, and the two of us would ride our Big Wheels down those hills and shoot directly across the road into each other's driveways, most of the time without looking.

Every other day, someone would have to slam on their brakes and come to a squealing halt to avoid hitting one of us. Then some mom would come knocking on our door and shout at my parents, "He didn't even look! He just scooted out. I almost hit him!"

We never stopped doing it, though. We just kept on zipping across, back and forth, pulling the emergency brake and spinning to a stop right at each other's mailbox. Listen, if the Dukes of Hazzard did it, we attempted it on those Big Wheels.

There was nothing terribly difficult about my childhood—certainly nothing like Jo felt when she walked into the school cafeteria. I always joke that my name was Chip, and that was tough enough. But other than that I was this athletic kid with friends, and I thought I had a pretty good life.

My only problem, if you want to call it a problem, is that I just never fit society's mold, especially at school. I was always talking at inappropriate times. I was always getting in trouble with teachers who said I didn't do things right. I wasn't writing right. I wasn't staying inside the lines. There was always some structure that I just somehow couldn't fit my little brain into. (That probably doesn't come as a surprise to anyone who knows me either.)

I never thought of my dad as an entrepreneur per se. I thought of him more as a businessman. And yet I seemed to pick up the entrepreneurial spirit from somewhere early on. I remember having my mom drive me down to the tennis courts, where I'd sell juice boxes to the kids in summer camp. I obviously wasn't getting rich off of this little business, but it was fun, and it taught me a little about money and work.

My parents did teach me the value of a dollar—and of hard work too. We were always working together as a family, out in the yard or inside the house. That was the beginning of a thought that became a full-fledged goal after I graduated from college. I told myself that I was going to live the rest of my life as if it were Saturday.

I told that to Jo early on, and she was a bit put off by that. At one point she said to me, "Chip, life just isn't like that. Life isn't always Saturday." I realized I needed to clarify what that phrase meant to me—so I suppose I ought to clarify it here too.

When I was growing up, Saturdays weren't always easy for us. In our house, you didn't sleep in until noon and then go to the beach. We would wake up at seven thirty on Saturday mornings and pull weeds until eleven. Once we were all sweating our brains out, then out came the lemonade, or here came the Popsicles. Then it was usually back to work—cleaning the house, cleaning our rooms, maybe helping Dad with some project. But when evening came, we would pack up the car and go for a real treat.

A real treat to us sometimes just meant McDonald's for dinner. If it were a big treat, Mom and Dad would take us camping for the night, or maybe we'd go to a movie once in a while. Whatever it was, it was fun. And that's what Saturday came to mean to me.

For us, Saturdays weren't about work, even though we did a lot of work. They weren't about going to an office somewhere, or to school, and having the whole family separated for the whole day. Saturdays were less structured. They were about getting the work done so you could go jump in the pool or have an ice cream cone.

There was something about school that didn't work for me— something about the fact that you had to turn in these assignments and you had to be there exactly when they said or else there was some disciplinary effort. Even before I got out of college, I vividly remember thinking, *I'm gonna put up with this for as long as I have to. But the second I don't have to put up with it anymore, I'm out. And I'm gonna live every day for the rest of my life as if it's Saturday.*

There would be times in the coming years when I would be flat broke and think, *Maybe I messed up. I feel like I'm living every day as if it's Monday!* But that feeling would never last long. Whenever I've been down financially, I've just picked myself up and worked a little harder. And whether it's a little luck or God or a combination, everything seems to find a way of working itself out eventually.

One thing my dad would preach to us when it came to money was, "I'll provide your needs, but you have to take care of your wants." So once I was old enough, if I told my parents I wanted some new toy or gadget, they'd say, "Well, great. There's this lawn two doors down that we keep driving by and noticing that it needs to be mowed. What if you went and knocked on that guy's door and asked him if you could mow it. How much is this thing you're looking for?"

"Well, it's twelve bucks."

"Okay. Well, if you offered to mow it for five, it would only take you two or three weeks, and you could have it!"

They never said no or "quit asking." They just said, "If you want that thing, here's an idea as to how you can go earn it."

There were times when I chose to be the lazy kid and wouldn't bother. And there were other times when I decided I really wanted something, so I'd grab the lawn mower and head down the street, knocking on doors.

When I was in third grade, my parents moved us to the Dallas area. Dad sold his sporting goods business and wound up landing a good job with American Airlines. It was a real corporate kind of a job, but my dad still managed to put his family first. He'd be home around five-thirty every night, and right after dinner he'd be out in the driveway shooting hoops with my sister, who was into basketball. Sometimes they'd play until nine or ten o'clock at night.

When I got a little older, I really took to baseball, and Dad did the same thing with me. Every night and every weekend, he'd be out there pitching balls to me and teaching me to field grounders.

The thing is, I started to get good at it. Dad got a bit of a gleam in his eye, thinking I might be some kind of a star player. I loved seeing him get so excited about it, and that made me try even harder.

For my dad, achieving goals was basically a mathematical equation: "If you hit a hundred balls a day and you work out this many hours, this many times a week, then this is what happens and you win state championships."

I followed his advice and, lo and behold, A plus B really did equal C for me. If I did this, then I achieved that. I started to become the star player he envisioned. I received all sorts of accolades, and everybody thought I was the greatest thing ever.

In some ways it was easy. It was just this mathematical thing. It would help keep me on the straight and narrow as I got into high school too. When a buddy was going off to a party, I could easily walk away by saying, "Man, I'd love to go and have a few beers—I'm not gonna lie to you. But jeez, I gotta go take a hundred ground balls. If I don't take a hundred ground balls every day, then I don't make the state tournament, and then I don't get a scholarship to go play ball in college."

Being a star athlete in high school sort of automatically buys you a lot of friends and attention. I was always the guy who had funny stories to tell, so when I walked into the cafeteria at Grapevine High School, everybody was calling me to come over to their table and eat with them. I just led a charmed life.

But somehow, instead of taking that and just running with it like some kids do, I never let go of that spirit I had when I was little—that desire to lift people up along with me and help them out if I could. I made friends with a kid who had Down syndrome, grabbing him to come play football with us on a Saturday afternoon. One of my friends was an Asian boy who'd been adopted from Vietnam. I just always loved getting to know people, all kinds, even if they weren't athletes or in the "popular" crowd.

Some of these friends of mine lived in the same neighborhood I did, so naturally we all became close. It was easy to make friends with the kids who lived close by, but I didn't forget about them in the cafeteria or in the hallway just because things were "different" at school. It was just never like that for me. I didn't like being put in a certain box, and I didn't appreciate people doing that to my friends either.

Being a popular guy in school actually had its downside. Sometimes I just wanted a day off. I felt a lot of pressure to show up to friends' parties, and people were let down when I didn't make it or even if I left early. It was actually a lot to live up to.

He's not a bragger, so he won't say these things if I don't speak up here, but Chip was the football captain at the same time he was playing scholarship-worthy baseball in high school. He was also voted "Most Likely to Succeed," "Most Likely to Be the Next President"—whatever you think a charmed-life kid would have, he had it.

I did. That's true. But the pressure of being Mr. Perfect, Mr. All-American, Mr. Most-Liked, and Mr. Well-Dressed was a lot to take, especially since my grades weren't very good. I became sort of addicted to the applause and praise, even from my parents, and I just felt awful anytime I let anybody down. Honestly, when I didn't play so well in a game and I saw the disappointment on my dad's face, it was hard. He had such high hopes for me, and I wanted to live up to them.

In some ways it's as if I was the Zack Morris character in that teen series *Saved by the Bell*. I was that guy. And our school was that wholesome in a lot of ways too. When we got in trouble, it was for TP'ing the vice principal's house or something. It was all "Come on, guys; let's win a state championship" or "Do the right thing."

There were nearly seven hundred people in my graduating class, but there was very little in terms of drugs, at least as far as I was aware. There was plenty of alcohol around, but I was scared to death of getting caught, so I pretty much steered clear. I seemed to have this innate ability to do the right thing and somehow make it look cool simultaneously.

Then I wound up playing baseball at North Lake Junior College, and going to that school was just a complete culture shock. A lot of the kids who went to that school came from very different back-grounds and seemed to have very different worldviews. I was used to being around disciplined athletes who dedicated themselves to being the best they could be on and off the field. But at North Lake some of the best athletes on the team were the rowdiest dudes. Athletes who were much better than I was were doing all sorts of things they shouldn't have been doing at the parties we went to.

Interestingly enough, girls hung around that team almost like groupies, and I hadn't expected that kind of thing at a junior col-lege. It was eye-opening. I felt like I was an innocent *Leave it to Beaver* character from the 1950s watching this wild spectacle from the sidelines. I went on dates with pretty girls, and I hung out at the parties, but I just never got into the whole scene. I never fit in. That was a weird position to be in after feeling like the king of Grapevine High.

I did manage to make friends with a couple of guys who were more like me, and those friendships helped get me through that first year, but my heart just wasn't there. I got this little notebook and started journaling, writing songs, and sketching out business plans in it. I'd spend hours in my apartment writing down my thoughts and ideas in that thing. I'd never done that before, but it was strangely therapeutic. I wish I could actually find that notebook. I would love for Jo to see it since that's so fitting in her personality.

That was the only season in my life when I ever tried to do any of those artsy-type things. I was just trying to express something that needed to come out, I suppose. And I'm sure it was one way of dealing with my loneliness.

I wanted out of that junior college. And luckily enough, a recruiter for Baylor happened to be in the stands when I made one of the greatest plays of my entire baseball career. I was playing second base, and I made this diving grab on a shot hit between first and second base. Then somehow I twisted around as I slid through the dirt to make a monster throw and get the runner out at first.

That recruiter offered to get me into Baylor and to make sure I would have a spot in the athletic dorm. I honestly couldn't even tell you if they covered my books, because I didn't care. I took it. I was ready to leave North Lake and start fresh.

As it turned out, I loved Baylor. I loved being around all those rich kids, even if I was nothing like them. I loved the girls. I loved the campus. I wasn't a very good student, and I struggled to pass every semester. But I did fall in love with the city of Waco and started to see myself staying in that town pretty much forever, especially once I started mowing lawns.

It's funny. Here I was, at this prestigious school, playing baseball and studying business. But instead of daydreaming about the major leagues or running some Fortune 500 company, I found myself in class looking out the window at the guys mowing grass and wishing I could trade places with them.

My junior year at Baylor, I decided that was exactly what I was going to do. I wasn't going to quit school. I would stay and finish my degree in business. But I wanted to go out and make money like I did as a kid—and not just in the summertime, the way I did with the book company and the fireworks stands. I wanted to work while I was going to school, to get outdoors, to start my own business. And I knew I would have to give something up if I was going to find the time to do that.

Turned out, the thing I needed to give up gave up on me first. A new coach came to Baylor and decided he wanted to make some major changes, so I was gone, along with a bunch of other guys who were on partial scholarships. And just like that, everything changed.

My dad was all fired up about my transferring to another school and finding a scholarship, and a few of my baseball buddies would go on to do that with great success. But I wasn't interested in chasing baseball all over the country. I had already seen the writing on the wall. I was a good baseball player, but I wasn't good enough to turn it into a full-time career. It just wasn't meant to be. It was time to move on.

I dreaded telling my dad, though. He'd spent all those years throwing balls to me for hours and hours every day. He'd come to every single one of my games, going all the way back to when I was a little kid, and when I grew older he'd acted almost as my agent or manager when it came to talking to schools or considering my future in the sport. He was so proud of me, and knowing I was going to let him down was pretty hard for me.

I put off that conversation for as long as I could, just worrying and worrying myself to death over how he was going to react. When I finally told him, I had tears in my eyes. But my dad looked at me and said, "Son, I love you. If you're telling me baseball is out, then it's out. It's okay."

It was this beautiful conversation. He was concerned about what I was going to focus on. I was too! My whole life had been about baseball, and when he asked me what I wanted to do, I told him I had no idea.

I told him I wanted to go out and maybe earn some money and start up a little business, and all he said was that whatever I did, he hoped I was as dedicated to it as I'd been to baseball. He wanted me to go out and hit the proverbial hundred balls every day, to give it my all no matter what I was doing.

I just remember vividly, for the first time in my life, really knowing in my heart of hearts that my dad loved me no matter what. It wasn't tied to baseball. It wasn't tied to something I did or didn't do. It was just an awesome feeling to realize that. And to this day that is one of the best conversations I've ever had with my old man.

I think I learned another lesson that day too: Sometimes worrying about something is much worse than the actual thing you're worrying about. So really, what's the point in worrying?

TEN

FLIPPING OUT

By the time Chip and I met, he'd managed to combine these two conflicting sides of himself: the kid who steered clear of trouble and did the right thing, and the kid who rode his Big Wheel full speed into the street without looking both ways. I had never met anyone like him. It's funny to me to think that the whole opposites-attract thing might have been programmed into my DNA. Just as my outgoing mother was drawn to my quiet dad, I was this shy girl drawn to the super-outgoing Chip Gaines. And the fact that he owned a successful lawn and irrigation business and had made up his mind that he loved Waco and wanted to stay put was somehow a perfect fit with everything I knew I wanted myself.

Jo didn't even realize that the lawn and irrigation business I was running when we met was actually the third version of that business I had launched. I'd managed to start each of these lawn businesses from scratch, build a clientele, and then sell it lock, stock, and barrel— meaning clientele, equipment, and employees—to somebody else. And that was on top of getting into the business of buying houses as rental properties, plus a little corner wash-and-fold business that I'd started. I almost forgot to mention that.

It all began when I tracked down the owner of the lawn service that took care of Baylor's landscaping. Remember when I'd look out the window and wish I could trade places with the guy mowing the grass? Well, that guy worked for this man. His name was David. And when I asked him for a job, he didn't think twice—he just simply told me no.

David was this real interesting guy who lived in a loft apartment he'd built inside his lawn company's warehouse. You'd never guess by looking at him, but I swear he was worth millions of dollars. I chatted him up the way I chat lots of people up, and I wouldn't take no for an answer. I wanted to get a job cutting grass, to learn the trade from the inside out. So I asked him, "How did you get your start?"

He said, "I don't know. I quit school in the seventh grade and just started mowing grass."

I kept asking questions, and he kept answering. Turns out, he was a really, really smart guy, and he basically became a mentor to me. I grew to call him Uncle David, and it's almost like I was sitting at his feet, as if he were some old guy whittling a stick on a front porch, teaching me these million-dollar life lessons. So I was getting the academic side at Baylor and learning common sense from one of the most commonsense guys on the planet. It was the perfect education for me.

Oh, and he finally hired me. I was persistent, if nothing else. And I grew to love that man, even though he was hard on me. He wasn't a real encouraging guy by nature. As a matter of fact, he used to joke to all his buddies that hiring me "was like losing two of his best guys."

I didn't mind. I had always had thick skin—thick skin and a positive self-image—so it took a lot to shake me. But one day after having worked a few months under Uncle David, I was on campus mowing with his guys, and I saw a fraternity soccer game going on at the intramural fields a few blocks over. Well, like a dog after a squirrel, off I went to watch, leaving my Weed Eater right where it was. Time got away from me, and it got dark before I knew it. My heart dropped when I went back to find the guys all gone—and no sign of the Weed Eater.

That Weed Eater cost what I made in a month, so I knew I was in big trouble. I hitched a ride back to the shop, and with my tail between my legs I told him what had happened. He was upset, but more in an "I trusted you" kind of way. You know, like when your parents would tell you they were disappointed in you rather than yelling. It's almost worse.

David made it clear that if I ever did something like that again, I was gone, and I promised it wouldn't. Right then and there I grew up a little. I realized having fun was one thing, but jacking around on someone else's dime and being flat-out disrespectful was another. I promised myself I'd never disrespect someone that way again.

I must've done all right after that, because Uncle David and I rocked and rolled together for a whole year after that without a hitch. Then one day he said to me, "Son, you're smart. You're going to Baylor University. What are you doing working for me? Go start your own lawn business. You've already seen what we do. Go do it."

He sent me to an equipment company in town, and I priced everything out, and the total for what I needed to get started came to $5,000. I didn't have $5,000. They told me to go across the street to the bank and try to get a loan. So I crossed the street and met a banker named Carroll Fitzgerald.

I had learned a few basic things about putting together a business plan at Baylor, but I didn't think that was enough to get me a loan with no collateral or experience. Carroll didn't think so either. He quickly said no.

But I wouldn't let up. I was a perpetual salesperson. I talked Carroll's ear off, saying, "Look, I've got five lawns I can start tomorrow. That means I'll be making X amount of dollars. I'm gonna quadruple that in a few months, and you guys are gonna make every cent back plus our agreed-on interest. I promise."

Carroll finally gave in and lent me the money—my first $5,000 loan. I walked out of the bank, walked back across the street to the equipment company, and spent every last penny on the things I would need to get my business off the ground in a first-rate way.

I repaid that loan in six months.

I was so excited by the whole thing. I got hooked—hooked on starting businesses, hooked on borrowing money, all of it. I still joke with Carroll to this day that he created a monster. I love borrowing money!

That was my senior year of college. And over the course of the next few years, as I've said, I sold that business off more than once. I built it up to more than a hundred accounts, with a crew, equipment, and a truck. And then I sold it to somebody else who wanted to get into the business.

To be honest, I never made a ton of money off of it. I treated it more like a part-time thing, and I had a lot of expenses paying the crew and everything. But I basically flipped that business the way I'd later start flipping houses. There wasn't always a ton of profit, but it was enough to keep you in the game until you could hit a lick and do it all over again. I was well on my way to building it up and getting ready to sell it again right when I met Jo.

Chip had basically gone through this whole education in the real world of entrepreneurship, and he told me all of these stories as we were first dating. I was in awe. I'd never met anyone who was such a go-getter at such a young age or who did things in such an unconventional way. It was like every time he opened a door, he encountered another door, and another, and he just kept opening every door. In fact, it was his Uncle David who sold him the eleven-acre property on Third Street that would eventually allow us to launch Magnolia Homes.